A CELEBRATION

TOLKIEN:
A CELEBRATION

Collected Writings on a Literary Legacy

Edited by Joseph Pearce

Fount
An Imprint of HarperCollinsPublishers

Fount is an Imprint of
HarperCollins*Religious*
Part of HarperCollins*Publishers*
77–85 Fulham Palace Road, London W6 8JB

First published in Great Britain in 1999 by Fount

Compilation © 1999 Joseph Pearce

3 5 7 9 10 8 6 4 2

Joseph Pearce asserts the moral right to be
identified as the compiler of this work

A catalogue record for this book is available from the British Library

ISBN 0 00 628120 6

Printed and bound in Great Britain by
Omnia Books Limited, Glasgow

CONDITIONS OF SALE

Contents

PREFACE

The idea for this volume was born out of research for *Tolkien: Man and Myth*, my biographical and literary study of Tolkien. Throughout the course of my work on this biography I came across several excellent essays which had hitherto remained unpublished or else had only appeared in relatively obscure periodicals. It seemed to me that these merited a far wider readership and, thankfully, James Catford of HarperCollins agreed with me. With his support and encouragement, I set about obtaining further essays until the body of work encompassed in the following pages was assembled. Together they represent not only a fitting celebration of Tolkien's life and work but also a potent response and effective riposte to his critics.

Appropriately enough, the collection begins and ends with the personal reminiscences of two people who knew Tolkien well. The recollections of both George Sayer and Walter Hooper offer a rare insight into the character of the man behind the myth and will be welcomed by anyone interested in obtaining a greater understanding of the person responsible for 'the greatest book of the century'. Sandwiched between these delightful memoirs are twelve essays which explore the many facets of Tolkien's work. *The Lord of the Rings*, *The Silmarillion* and *The Hobbit* are examined theologically, philosophically, socio-politically, culturally, ecologically, mystically and historically as the various contributors seek to understand the profundity of Tolkien's achievement. Each essay draws deep draughts from the seemingly fathomless well of Tolkien's sub-creation and each is a testimony to the endurance of perennial wisdom in the face of the clichéd shallows of modern criticism. Above all, the collection of essays contained in this volume represents a fitting celebration of both the man and the myth behind *The Lord of the Rings*.

ACKNOWLEDGEMENTS

First and foremost I must acknowledge the various contributors to this volume: George Sayer, Stratford Caldecott, Patrick Curry, Robert Murray SJ, Charles A. Coulombe, James V. Schall SJ, Elwin Fairburn, Kevin Aldrich, Colin Gunton, Richard Jeffery, Stephen R. Lawhead, Sean McGrath and Walter Hooper. Every effort has been made to contact these writers and, in the cases where this has not been possible, full acknowledgement will be given in future editions of this work. I would like to thank those contributors who have kindly granted permission for their work to be included and I offer particular thanks to those who have written essays for this volume at my specific request. An extra debt of gratitude is due to Stratford Caldecott at the Centre for Faith and Culture in Oxford who first introduced me to some of these essays when I sought his assistance in the course of research for *Tolkien: Man and Myth*, my literary life of Tolkien. I am also grateful to Walter Hooper for granting me the interview and for the hospitality he always shows me on my visits to his home in Oxford. Similar gratitude is due to Aidan and Dorene Mackey who continue to show me the greatest kindness whenever I impose upon them. Other long-suffering friends who never fail to offer assistance whenever required include Alfred Simmonds and Sarah Hollingsworth.

Finally, I acknowledge HarperCollins for permission to quote from Tolkien's work and, more particularly, to James Catford for his continuing faith in my literary endeavours.

Dedication to Owen Barfield
1898–1997
The First Inkling

If 1998 marked the twenty-fifth anniversary of Tolkien's death and the centenary of C. S. Lewis's birth, it also marked the centenary of the birth of Owen Barfield, the first and often forgotten Inkling.

Owen Barfield, who died in December 1997 shortly after his ninety-ninth birthday, deserves a place of honour alongside his good friends C. S. Lewis and J. R. R. Tolkien and, for this reason, this volume in celebration of Tolkien is dedicated to his memory.

I had the good fortune of meeting Mr Barfield on 31 December 1996, on the eve of what would be his last New Year. He had kindly agreed to see me after I had sought his assistance for my study of twentieth-century literary converts. In spite of his failing health he granted me a delightful interview at his home in Forest Row in which he shared many memories of a literary world which had long since disappeared. He recalled attending a debate between Chesterton and Shaw at a theatre in London, and spoke of several meetings with T. S. Eliot, including having tea with Eliot and Walter de la Mare at the latter's 'rather nice flat' in Putney. Most memorable of all were the stories about his friendship with Lewis and Tolkien. He spoke of discussing Chesterton with Lewis, and recalled reading the whole of the *Iliad*, the whole of the *Odyssey* and the whole of the *Divine Comedy* with Lewis. He also remembered with evident affection long walks with Lewis and Dom Bede Griffiths.

I am grateful for having met Owen Barfield whose *Poetic Diction: A Study in Meaning* exerted such a profound influence on both Tolkien and Lewis following its publication in 1928. During my all too brief encounter with him and in spite of his magisterial age, he still displayed glimpses of the genius which had impressed his more famous friends almost sixty years earlier.

'I'm not an old man, I'm a very old man,' he had told Walter Hooper when Mr Hooper visited him on his ninety-eighth birthday scarcely seven weeks before my own visit. Shortly afterwards he told Mr Hooper, with characteristic wit, that 'I'm not getting on, I'm getting off.' A few months later, he did indeed 'get off', leaving those who met him with many fond memories of a world which seemed to have passed away with him. *Requiescat in pace.*

RECOLLECTIONS OF J. R. R. TOLKIEN
GEORGE SAYER

George Sayer was head of the English Department at Malvern College from 1949 until 1974 and, as an undergraduate many years earlier, was a pupil of C. S. Lewis at Magdalen College, Oxford. He became one of Lewis's closest friends and is author of Jack: C. S. Lewis and His Times. *He was also a good friend of Tolkien and these reminiscences, first delivered and subsequently published as part of the Proceedings of the J. R. R. Tolkien Centenary Conference in 1992, represent a celebration of that friendship. They also form an appropriate introduction to this celebration of Tolkien's life and work.*

On earth Ronald Tolkien loved parties, so I think he'll be there among the immortals enjoying this imaginative and beautifully organized centenary party. One or two items on the menu may surprise him – for instance why should mushrooms or morels, homely English things, be translated into French, not at all his favourite language? But that's a detail. I hope nothing I say will offend him if he bothers to listen, that all I say about him will be worthy of the great courtesy and kindness he always showed me.

I got to know him through C. S. Lewis, who was my tutor when I read English at Magdalen. Lewis took a low view of the standard of lecturing in Oxford – a view that was, I think, correct. He advised me to go only to two-and-a-half series of lectures in first year. The two were his own lectures and those of Nevill Coghill. The half was Tolkien's. 'I don't know what to say about Tolkien,' was how he put it.

> He is scholarly, and he can be brilliant though perhaps rather recondite for most undergraduates. But unfortunately you may not be able to hear what he says. He is a bad lecturer. All the same I advise you to go. If you do, arrive early, sit near the front and pay particular attention to the extempore remarks and comments he often makes. These are usually the best things in the lecture. In fact one could call him an inspired speaker of footnotes.

'An inspired speaker of footnotes.' INSPIRED. The word stuck in my mind, but it was not until many years later that I realized that Lewis was saying something profoundly true about Tolkien's writing as well as his lecturing. He really is an inspired writer. The general level of his work is high and every now and then one comes across passages and whole incidents of real inspiration. The Ents are an example. They are a wonderful invention that owes, as far as I know, nothing to previous writing. They are like nothing else that has ever been. They are charming and lovable with, also, the sadness characteristic of the author, a sadness that underlies much of his humour. Another example is the ride to Gondor where the prose narrative rises to the truly heroic, the rarest thing in modern literature and perhaps the literary quality that its author admired most. What one could call very good footnotes sometimes occurred in his private conversation. If he was with several other people and not very interested in what they were talking about, he might mutter to whoever sat nearest him a comment that was, as far as one could hear it, of real interest.

But in spite of the footnotes, I was disappointed in Tolkien's lectures. Unlike Lewis, who had a fine resonant voice, he had a poor voice and made things worse by mumbling. I did try arriving early and sitting in the front. I then found myself sitting in the midst of a small group of young women who knew each other rather well. At least some of them must have gone to him for tutorials. I think that in the early days the women's colleges sent him pupils because he was a married man. If he had not been, a woman undergraduate would not have been allowed to go to a tutorial with him alone. She would have had to be chaperoned by another woman. I think he retained this connection with women's colleges after the demise or neglect of the chaperoning rule.

I noticed that some of them spoke of him with affection, as 'rather sweet'. The more homely enjoyed going to his north Oxford house and meeting the little Tolkiens, as I heard them called, presumably Christopher and Priscilla. I followed the good example of those around me and tried to take notes. This wasn't easy for he went quite fast. The footnotes were for me certainly the best part but there were not enough of them and I enjoyed them for wrong or quite unintellectual reasons, because in them Tolkien showed a rather pleasant sense of humour. But in spite of these I foolishly soon gave up going. Since this may shock those of you who do not know Oxford and Cambridge, I had better explain that going to lectures was entirely voluntary at these ancient universities. It still is, and is unnecessary too for success in Schools. My stepdaughter, Sheena, who was recently up at St John's, never went to a single lecture all the time she was up. Yet she got a first.

My real relationship with Tolkien did not begin until about thirteen years later. It was during the school holidays at Malvern where I was teaching. Quite near the college I came across C. S. Lewis and his brother Warren apparently setting out for a hike. They were wearing open-neck shirts, very old clothes, had stout walking sticks, and one of them was carrying a very ancient looking rucksack. It was the fact that they were doing it in Malvern that surprised me because I know that C. S. Lewis was certainly not the old-boy type, even though his brother was. They explained that they had swopped houses with Maureen, Mrs Moore's daughter, who had married Leonard Blake, the Director of Music at Malvern College. She had gone to Lewis's house, The Kilns, to be with her mother, who was ill. With them was Tolkien and a man whom they introduced to me as Humphrey Havard, 'our friend and doctor'. Lewis invited me to have some beer with them at the pub called The Unicorn. There he asked me which were the best walks in the area, and then if I could join them for the next few days, acting as their guide. Lewis then drew me on one side and said that they would be extremely grateful if I would be willing to walk much of the time with Tolkien, while they went on ahead.

> He's a great man, but not our sort of walker. He doesn't seem able to talk and walk at the same time. He dawdles and then stops completely when he has something interesting to say. Warnie finds this particularly irritating.

I soon found that the brothers liked to walk hard and fast for half an hour, a period which Warnie would time, for Jack never wore or, as far as I know, owned a watch. Then they would have what they called a 'soak'. This meant sitting or lying down for the time it took to have a cigarette. Then the other man would shoulder the pack, which was their name for the rucksack, and they would go on walking hard for another half-hour. Humphrey Havard had been most kind in walking some of the time with Tolkien but he had to go back to Oxford the following day.

It worked really well. Tolkien seemed glad to be left behind by the Lewis brothers, whom he described to me as 'ruthless walkers, very ruthless indeed'. Certainly he was not used to their sort of walking, and got quickly out of breath when we walked uphill. Just as C. S. Lewis said, he tended to stop walking, certainly walking fast, whenever he had something interesting to say. He also liked to stop to look at the trees, flowers, birds and insects that we passed. He would not have suited anyone who, like the Lewis brothers, walked partly for health, in order to get vigorous exercise. But it delighted me. He talked so well that I was happy to do nothing but listen, though even if one was by his side, it was not always easy to hear all that he said. He talked faster than anyone of his age that I have known, and in a curious fluttering way. Then he would often spring from one topic to another, or interpolate remarks that didn't seem to have much connection with what we were talking about. He knew more natural history than I did, certainly far more than the Lewises, and kept coming out with pieces of curious information about the plants that we came across. I can remember one or two examples. Thus on the common wood avens:

> This is Herb Bennet, in Latin *Herba Benedicta*. What do you think that means?
> The Blessed Plant.
> Yes, though the English form wants it to be *St Benedict's Herb*. It is blessed because it is a protection from the devil. If it is put into a house 'the devil can do nothing, and if a man carries it about with him no venomous beast will come within scent of it'.

And upon the celandine:

> Did you know that when picking celandine various combinations of *Aves* and *Paternosters* have to be said? This was one of the many cases of Christian prayers supplanting pagan ones, for in ancient times there were runes to be spoken before it was picked.

Though he was generally interested in birds and insects, his greatest love seemed to be for trees. He had loved trees ever since childhood. He would often place his hand on the trunks of ones that we passed. He felt their wanton or unnecessary felling almost as murder. The first time I heard him say 'ORCS' was when he heard not far off the savage sound of a petrol-driven chainsaw. 'That machine,' he said, 'is one of the greatest horrors of our age.' He said that he had sometimes imagined an uprising of the trees against their human tormentors. 'Think of the power of a forest on the march. Of what it would be like if Birnam Wood really came to Dunsinane.'

I had the impression that he had never walked the hills before though he had often admired the distant view of them from the Avon valley near Evesham. Some of the names of the places we saw from the hills produced philological or etymological footnotes. *Malvern* was a corruption of two Welsh words, 'moel' meaning *bear*, and 'vern' derived from *bryn* or *fryn* meaning *hill*. This of course told us that the area was in early times heavily wooded, though the ten-mile ridge of the hills was not. The main pass over the hills is called the Wyche. This gave him an opportunity of talking about the various meanings of the word 'Wyc'.

It was the custom of the Lewis brothers to eat the bread and cheese they brought with them in a pub and to drink with it a couple of pints of beer, always bitter. They liked the beer to be drawn from the wood and the pub to be simple, primitive and above all without a radio. Tolkien agreed strongly with this taste. I can think of a pub he wouldn't enter because there was a radio on. But he was happy drinking beer, or smoking his pipe in a pub among friends.

Usually he was genial and relaxed, as if liberated from the worries of ordinary life. As I sat with him and the Lewis brothers in the pub, I remember being fascinated by the expressions on his face, the way they changed to suit what he was saying. Often he was smiling, genial, or wore a pixy look. A few seconds later he might burst into savage scathing criticism, looking fierce and menacing. Then he might soon become genial again. There was an element of acting about this gesturing, but much that he said was extremely serious.

Except at Inklings meetings I saw nothing of Tolkien for perhaps two years after this. Lewis gave me bulletins about him, and talked quite a lot about *The Lord of the Rings*, its greatness and the difficulty of getting it published. He thought this was largely Tolkien's fault because he insisted that it should be published with a lengthy appendix of largely philological interest. In negotiation with Collins he had even gone so far as to insist that it should be published with the earlier book, *The Silmarillion*, a book that Lewis had tried to read in typescript, but found very heavy going. The two together would make a volume of over a million words. Even alone *The Lord of the Rings* would, Lewis thought, be the better for pruning. There was a large section that in his opinion weakened the book.

Of course Lewis's enthusiasm made my wife and me most eager to read the book. Lewis said that he would try and get a copy for us, but he did not see how. Then on one of my visits to Magdalen he told me that Tolkien had given up hope of ever having it published. This was a real calamity, but it brought great good to me. 'Look,' he said, 'at what I have here for you!' There on his table was the typescript of *The Lord of the Rings*. Of course I must take the greatest care of it, read it in a month or less, and return it personally to the author, phoning him first to make sure that he would be there to receive it. It was far too precious to be entrusted even to the more reliable post of forty years ago.

Of course my wife and I had the thrilling experience that all of you remember vividly. Well before the month was up, I turned up with it at Tolkien's house, then in Holywell. I found him obviously unhappy and dishevelled. He explained that his wife had gone to Bournemouth and that all his friends were out of Oxford. He eagerly accepted my invitation to come to Malvern for a few days. 'But what shall I do with the other book? I can't leave it here.' So I drove Tolkien to Malvern with the typescripts of *The Lord of the Rings* and *The Silmarillion* on the back seat. What a precious cargo!

His talk now was mainly of his books. He had worked for fourteen years on *The Lord of the Rings* and before that for many years on *The Silmarillion*. They really were his life work. He had in a sense planned them before he went to school, and actually written one or two of the poems while he was still at school, I think the Tom Bombadil poems. He had now nothing to look forward to except a life of broken health, making do on an inadequate pension. He was so miserable and so little interested in anything except his own troubles that we were seriously worried. What could we do to alleviate his depression? I could walk with him and drive him around during the day, but how were we to get through the evenings? Then I had an idea. I would take the risk of introducing him to a new machine that I had in the house and was trying out because it seemed that it should have some valuable education applications. It was a large black box, a Ferrograph, an early-model tape recorder. To confront him with it was a risk because he had made it clear that he disliked all machinery. He might curse it and curse me with it, but there was a chance that he would be interested in recording on it, in hearing his own voice.

He was certainly interested. First he recorded the Lord's Prayer in Gothic to cast out the devil that was sure to be in it since it was a machine. This was not just whimsy. All of life for him was part of a cosmic conflict between the forces of good and evil, God and the devil. I played it back to him. He was surprised and very pleased. He sounded much better than he had expected. He went on to record some of the poems in *The Lord of the Rings*. Some he sang to the tunes that were in his head when writing them. He was delighted with the result. It was striking how much better his voice sounded recorded and amplified. The more he recorded, and the more often he played back the recordings, the more his confidence grew. He asked to record the great riddle scene from *The Hobbit*. He read it magnificently and was especially pleased with his impersonation of Gollum. Then I suggested he should read one or two of the best prose passages from *The Lord of the Rings*, say, the 'Ride of the Rohirrim', and part of the account of the events on Mount Doom. He listened carefully and, I thought, nervously, to the play-back. 'You know,' he said, 'they are all wrong. The publishers are wrong, and I am wrong to have lost my faith in my own work. I am sure this is good, really good. But how am I to get it published?'

Of course I had no idea. But I had to say something, so I said, 'Haven't you an old pupil in the publishing business?' After a pause he said: 'There's only Rayner.' 'Then send it to him and ask for his help.'

I won't tell you what happened after that because you would have heard it from Rayner Unwin himself.

He went on recording until I ran out of tape.

Of course compared with this nothing in my relationship with Tolkien is of much importance, but I will tell you a few other things. I don't think he much liked the food he had while staying with us, because my wife was then working through a French cookery book, and he seemed to detest everything French – I don't know why. We thought he had a bad appetite. Nevertheless he thanked her with a charming bread-and-butter letter written in Elvish and complete with English translation.

While with us he asked if he could do something to help in the house or garden. He was quite domesticated, not at all an impractical academic. We thought, in the garden, for our garden has never been a tidy or weed-free one. He chose an area of about two square yards, part flower border and part lawn and cultivated it perfectly: the border meticulously weeded and the soil made level and exceedingly fine; the grass cut with scissors closely and evenly. It took him quite a long time to do the job, but it was beautifully done. He was in all things a perfectionist. I think his training in domesticity, in housework, gardening, and looking after chickens and other creatures gave to his writing a homely and earthy quality. On Sunday we took him to Mass at the church to which we always go ourselves. Before we left the house he asked if confessions were heard before Mass. I told him they were. He said he always liked to go to confession before receiving communion. I do not think that this was because he had on his conscience any sin that most people would regard as serious. True, he was what spiritual directors call 'scrupulous', that is, inclined to exaggerate the evil of the undisciplined and erring thoughts that plague most of us. But he was above all a devout and strict old-fashioned Catholic, who had been brought up to think that if possible one should go to confession first. This was the usual nineteenth-century attitude. It lingered in backward parts. Thus my wife tells me that in her village in County Kerry in the 1930s, no one would have thought of going to communion without going to confession first. In the pew in front of us there were two or three children who were trying to follow the service in a simple picture-book missal. He seemed to be more interested in them than in events at the altar. He lent over and helped them. When we came out of the church we found that he was not with us. I went back and found him kneeling in front of the Lady Altar with the young children and their mother, talking happily and I think telling stories about Our Lady. I knew the mother and found out later that they were enthralled. This again was typical; he loved children and had the gift of getting on well with them. 'Mummy, can we always go to church with that nice man?' The story also illustrates one of the most important things about him, his great devotion to Our Lady. He wrote to me years later a letter in which he stated that he attributed anything that was good or beautiful in his writing to the influence of Our Lady, 'the greatest influence in my life'. He meant it. An obvious example is the character of Galadriel.

The few days he spent in Malvern with that early-model Ferrograph tape recorder at a time when he was 'in the doldrums' as he put it in a letter, made me one of his friends. He invited me to call on him whenever I was in Oxford and with remarkable frankness talked to me not merely about *The Lord of the Rings* and his other writings but about his private worries about things such as money, religion and family.

In the spring of 1953 he moved to Sandfield Road, a turning on Headington Hill off the London Road. I think that when I called, it was always Mrs Tolkien who answered the door. One of her jobs was to protect her husband from people who would interfere with his work. She would then go upstairs to tell him that I, an admissible visitor, was there. I always found him seated at a large desk or table with many papers in front of him in a room full of books and piles of papers. I was told that there was also a bookstore and a sort of office in what would have been the garage if he had had a car. Until *The Lord of the Rings* was a success he talked a good deal about his misfortunes. He had much to complain about. The expenses of the move had made him rather short of money, and yet he would have to contribute more than he could afford towards publication of *The Lord of the Rings*. Perhaps the best way of conveying his state of mind will be to read a few sentences about his anxieties from a letter he wrote to me at the end of August, 1953. It also shows that he had taken with enthusiasm to the use of a tape recorder:

> When I got your letter I was altogether played out. Not that I have been able to relax, beyond one morning's long sleep.

Life has been most complicated and laborious with domestic comings and goings and difficulties arranging for Father John and anxieties about my daughter lost in France. Amidst all this I have had to work day and (especially) night at the seemingly endless galleys of the Great Work that had piled up during Vivas, at drawings and runes and maps; and now at the copy of Vol. II. Also at Sir Gawain.

Immediately after Vivas Newby of the Talks Department descended on me. The upshot is that my translation is being taken in toto, uncut, as the basis of six broadcasts at Christmas. But they do not take equally kindly to me as the actual performer. However I go to London tomorrow for an audition. This is where a tape-recorder would have been so helpful. I had to hire a horrid old sound Mirror, the best I could get locally, but it was very helpful in matters of timing and speed. With the help of Christopher and Faith, I made some three voice experiments and recordings of the temptation scenes. An enormous improvement – and assistance to the listener. Chris was making an extremely good (if slightly Oxonian) Gawain, before we had to break off.

I got as near to Malvern as Evesham on August 23rd. The wedding of my nephew Gabriel Tolkien, at which John officiated. I thought not without longing of the Dark Hills in the distance, but I had to rush straight back.

He doubted if many people would buy the book at the high price of 25 shillings a volume. He feared too that the few people who read it would treat it as an allegory or morality about the nuclear bomb or the horrors of the machine age. He insisted over and over again that his book was essentially a story, without any further meaning. 'Tales of Faerie,' he said, 'should be told only for their own sake.'

One of the advantages of the house in Sandfield Road was that Tolkien's doctor, Humphrey Havard, lived in the same street, only a few doors away. He sometimes took him to church. I once asked him how he was and had the answer:

> All right now, but I've been in a very bad state. Humphrey came here and told me that I must go to confession and that he would come early on Sunday morning to take me to confession and communion. That's the sort of doctor to have.

This story shows his humility. He had a very low opinion of his own merits, and fairly easily got into a depressed state when thinking of his faults and deficiencies. Life was a war between good and evil. He thought the sacraments freed one from enthralment to Sauron. Once he spoke to me of Ireland after he had spent part of a summer vacation working there as an examiner: 'It is as if the earth there is cursed. It exudes an evil that is held in check only by Christian practice and the power of prayer.' Even the soil, the earth, played a part in the cosmic struggle between forces of good and evil.

He thought hatred of Catholics was common in Britain. His mother, to whom he was most deeply devoted, was a martyr because of her loyalty to the Catholic faith, and his wife, Edith, was turned out of her guardian's house when she was received into the Church. In 1963 he wrote in a letter:

> And it still goes on. I have a friend who walked in procession in the Eucharistic Congress in Edinburgh, and who reached the end with a face drenched with spittle of the populace which lined the road and were only restrained by mounted police from tearing the garments and faces of the Catholics.

He found little or nothing wrong with the pre-Vatican II Church, and therefore thought the reforms of the 1960s misguided and unnecessary. He frequently complained about the new English translations of the Latin texts used in Catholic services, because they were inaccurate or in bad or clumsy English.

Lewis told Tolkien that of all his friends he was 'the only one impervious to influence'. This was largely true. It was no defect. Combined with his belief in all the traditional virtues such as courage, loyalty, chastity, integrity and kindness, it gave him as a man and to *The Lord of the Rings* tremendous moral strength. He was unswervingly loyal to the Christian faith as taught him by his guardian and benefactor, Father Francis Morgan.

Our mutual friend, C. S. Lewis, was a frequent topic of conversation. Their relationship before the war had been very close, so close that Edith Tolkien had resented the time that her husband spent with him. Lewis, who was aware of this, for his part found it impossible to see as much as he would have liked of Tolkien, whom he described as 'the most married man he knew'. But apart from the fact that one of them was married, the two had different concepts of friendship. Tolkien wanted to be first among Lewis's friends. Lewis may have loved Tolkien as much but he wanted him to be one among several friends. Tolkien was jealous of the position that Charles Williams, of whom he did not entirely approve, occupied in Lewis's affections. They were separated also by the success of the Narnia stories, the first of which appeared when he was struggling to get *The Lord of the Rings* through the press. He described it to be 'about as bad as can be'. It was written superficially and far too quickly (I think that perhaps he envied Lewis his fluency), had an obvious message, but above all was a mix-up of characters from dissimilar and incompatible imaginative worlds. Dr Cornelius, Father Time, the White Witch, Father Christmas and Dryads should not be included in the same story. I never saw the force of this criticism.

At long last, after the three volumes were successfully launched, he became what Lewis called 'cock-a-hoop' and talked with great enthusiasm of the fate of the pirated paper-back version and the astonishing growth of the Tolkien cult. He enjoyed receiving letters in Elvish from boys at Win-chester and from knowing that they were using it as a secret language. He was overwhelmed by his fan mail and would-be visitors. It was wonderful to have at long last plenty of money, more than he knew what to do with. He once began a meeting with me by saying: 'I've been a poor man all my life, but now for the first time I've a lot of money. Would you like some?'

In my later visits he was nominally hard at work getting *The Silmarillion* into a form suitable for publication. But after a time I began to wonder how much he really did. I can think of two visits at an interval of a month. On the second I am almost sure that he had the same page open as on the first. I have been told that he spent much of his time reading detective stories. I don't blame him. His life work was complete.

I once asked him about the origin of *The Silmarillion* and *The Lord of the Rings*. It seemed to be more than anything else philological. Then just as I was leaving to go on a walk with C. S. Lewis he handed me a pile of papers. 'If you're interested, have a look at these.'

Lewis and I took them to a pub and looked at them over bread and cheese. 'Good Heavens!' he exclaimed, 'he seems to have invented not one but three languages complete with their dialects. He must be the cleverest man in Oxford. But we can't keep them. Take them straight back to him while I have another pint.'

If I was there at the right time in the afternoon he would take me to have tea in the drawing room on the floor below, Edith Tolkien's room. The atmosphere was quite different, with hardly any papers and few books. She did most of the talking and it was not at all literary. Frequent subjects were the doings of the children, especially Christopher, the grandchildren, the garden in which I think Ronald enjoyed working, the iniquities of the Labour Party, the rising price of food, the changes for the worse in the Oxford shops and the difficulty of buying certain groceries. The road had deteriorated since they had moved there. It used to be a quiet cul-de-sac. Now the lower end had been opened up and lorries and cars rushed through on their way to a building site or to Oxford United's football ground. There were also some very noisy people in the road. They even had as near neighbours an aspiring pop group.

Ronald (I call him Ronald in talking to you, but I always addressed him by his Inklings nickname, 'Tollers') told me that when she was younger Edith had been a fine pianist. Some of the conversation was about music. On one occasion she played to us on a very simple old-fashioned gramophone a record that she had just bought. Her husband was relaxed and happy with this domesticity. Anyway, it was an important part of his life. Without a liking for the homely and domestic, he could not have written *The Hobbit*, or invented Frodo and Sam Gamgee, characters that sustain quite convincingly the story of *The Lord of the Rings*, and link the high romance to the everyday and the ordinary.

He told me that he was moving to Bournemouth because the house was too big and too much work for Edith, and in order to escape the fan mail and the fans. I did not go there. The last time I met him was after his return to Oxford. He was with children (perhaps great-grandchildren), playing trains: 'I'm Thomas the Tank Engine. Puff. Puff. Puff.' That sort of thing. I was conscripted as a signal. This love for children and delight in childlike play and simple pleasures was yet another thing that contributed to his wholeness as a man and the success of his books.

2

OVER THE CHASM OF FIRE:
CHRISTIAN HEROISM IN THE SILMARILLION
AND THE LORD OF THE RINGS
STRATFORD CALDECOTT

Stratford Caldecott is Director of the Centre for Faith & Culture in Oxford, Assistant Editor of The Chesterton Review *and Acting Director of the European branch of the G. K. Chesterton Institute. He is on the Editorial Board of the International Catholic Review* Communio, *and editor of the book* Beyond the Prosaic: Renewing the Liturgical Movement *(T&T Clark, 1998). He is married to the writer Léonie Caldecott: they have three children.*

'Book of the Century' *The Lord of the Rings* is the work of a devout Catholic. Its Elvish chants are strung on melodic lines redolent of Benediction, and its moral structure comes straight out of the New Testament. This is, then, a Christian work, albeit of a genre both ages old and at the same time brilliantly original. As we move from the opening chapters set in the Shire to the wider canvas of Middle-earth, *The Lord of the Rings* manages to integrate the form of the modern novel back into the much longer tradition of epic poetry and heroic saga. Not that Tolkien was a professional bard, praising the deeds of his tribal chief or embellishing ancient legends in some smoky castle. He was an Oxford don, a professor of languages who had to write his stories alone, deep into the night, and at the risk of his daytime reputation. The nearest he got to campfire or castle hall was the smoke-filled bar of the Eagle and Child tavern, and there with his friends the Inklings he did indeed reveal himself at home in the age-old oral tradition.

The Lord of the Rings is not a flawless work, but it is richer and deeper than many books more carefully crafted by shallower men. What drove Tolkien so deep into the night was not merely the desire to tell a story, but the awareness that he was *part* of a story. He may have been writing fiction, but he was *telling the truth* about the world as it revealed itself to him. And this truth he discovered as he wrote, through the very process of writing. 'I always had the sense of recording what was already "there", somewhere: not of "inventing",' (*Letters*, p. 131); a feeling that lay behind the fictional device of the 'Red Book of Westmarch' on which *The Lord of the Rings* was supposedly based. In a letter to his son Christopher he admitted: 'the thing seems to write itself once I get going, as if the truth comes out then, only imperfectly glimpsed in the preliminary sketch' (*Letters*, p. 91). It was a truth about himself ('I have exposed my heart to be shot at,' he writes in *Letters*, p. 142), but one profound enough to be at the same time a truth about us, and about each of those millions of readers. 'After all,' he wrote, 'I believe that legends and myths are largely made of "truth", and indeed present aspects of it that can only be perceived in this mode; and long ago certain truths and modes of this kind were discovered and must always reappear' (*Letters*, p. 131). This is a belief that Tolkien shared not only with the Inklings, but with their great forerunner, George MacDonald, and the entire Romantic Movement.

In a draft letter to an admirer dated 1971, Tolkien writes of his great work, 'It was written slowly and with great care for detail, & finally emerged as a Frameless Picture: a searchlight, as it were, on a brief period in History, and on a small part of our Middle-earth, surrounded by the glimmer of limitless extensions in time and space. Very well: that may explain to some extent why it "feels" like history; why it was accepted for publication; and why it has proved readable for a large number of very different kinds of people. But it does not fully explain what has actually happened. Looking back on the wholly unexpected things that have followed its publication – beginning at once with the appearance of Vol. I – I feel as if an ever darkening sky over our present world had been suddenly pierced, the clouds rolled back, and an almost forgotten sunlight had poured down again. As if indeed the horns of Hope had been heard again, as Pippin heard them suddenly at the absolute *nadir* of the fortunes of the West. But *How?* and *Why?*' (*Letters*, p. 328). He goes on to describe how once he encountered Gandalf, in the person of a man who visited him to discuss certain old pictures that seemed almost designed to illustrate *The Lord of the Rings*. The man remarks after a silence: 'Of course you don't suppose, do you, that you wrote all that book yourself?'

I know a Catholic priest who reads all the way through *The Lord of the Rings* once a year. Why would someone do that? Of course, people can get obsessed about anything that takes them out of themselves (I recently read of a mother and daughter who claimed to have been to see the movie *Titanic* forty-eight times). But my priest friend is not like that – and nor was I, when I read the book over and over again as I was growing up. The 'truth' in myths and legends bears repeating because it cannot be taken in all at once. There are stories that we have to *grow into*; stories that deal with the way the world is made, and the way the Self is made. These stories are like dreams, but dreams that can be shared by an entire culture; wholesome dreams that restore a balance to the psyche by turning our energies and our thoughts towards truth; dreams that resemble an oasis in the desert. Reading them can be a bit like praying. 'Finally, brethren, whatever is true, whatever is honourable, whatever is just, whatever is lovely, whatever is gracious, if there is any excellence, if there is anything worthy of praise, consider these things' (Philippians 4:8).

The Lord of the Rings is about a Quest, but the writing of it was also a Quest, and the reading of it can be likewise. The

Quest, of course, is one of the three or four 'deep structures' used by storytellers the world over. A Quest is any journey in which some difficult goal is to be achieved, some challenge must be met, some initiation has to be undergone, some place or object or person is to be discovered or won. The reason for its perennial popularity is obvious enough. It is just such a Quest that gives meaning to our own existence. We are not where (or whom) we wish to be: to get there it is necessary to travel – even if, as G. K. Chesterton and T. S. Eliot knew so well, we travel only to arrive back at our beginning, 'And know the place for the first time' (*Little Gidding*). We read or listen to the storyteller, then, in order to orient ourselves for this journey within. We want to learn how to behave, in order to get *where we want to go*. Each of us knows, deep down inside, that our life is not merely a mechanical progress from cradle to grave; it is a search for something, for some elusive treasure. The same ultimate goal motivates us in both work and play. What the storyteller depends upon is a fact of human nature: that our imagination is always reaching out beyond the limits of the known and the evident, towards the infinity of what is desired. The Quest activates our nostalgia for paradise lost, our yearning for the restoration or fulfilment to come.

The book we know as *The Lord of the Rings* is only a fragment of a much larger set of tales, most of which were not published during Tolkien's lifetime. Over the years he added to them layer by layer, filling in a vast historical canvas, weaving theme upon theme, until the whole collection resembled a great 'tree of tales', seemingly as ancient as a gnarled oak. It may not have been the 'mythology for England' that he once dreamed of creating (see *Letters*, p. 131), but the phrase suggests one part of his intention. He was exploring the archetypes and images of a people – his own people of northern and western Europe. Each particular story had to appear to belong to a much larger and more ancient body of literature in order to evoke the symbolic resonances without which it would fail to cast its spell. There had to be a sense of great vistas of time and space around and behind each story, as there is in the legends of a people like the Norsemen or the Celts, each of which comes down to us out of its own tremendous 'mythic space', an imaginal dimension where dramatic action 'interprets eternity to time and time to eternity' (if I may quote my mother, the folklorist Moyra Caldecott).

To discover such a mythic space, Tolkien had to go in search of the very springs of the imagination. As C. S. Lewis put it, he had to penetrate a kind of 'veil' to the inner core of human creativity, into the place where *language* is born. He had to go 'inside language'. The artificial languages we encounter in his work were therefore not developed merely to decorate his stories, or to create the illusion of authenticity – although they certainly do function that way. More importantly, the stories and the languages emerged from the same source and at the same time. The stories were born first as poetry; only later as prose. This is as it should be, for of the two forms, poetry is the more concentrated and direct expression of experience.

As a philologist, Tolkien was well prepared for his personal Quest. Already at school he had taught himself nearly a dozen languages. And as a Christian, he knew that 'In the beginning was the Word ... In him was life, and the life was the light of men.' His own mythology begins with the creation. The One God, Ilúvatar, brings the world into existence with the word '*Eä*! Let these things Be!', sending into the void the Flame Imperishable. Behind the actual moment of creation lies the Music of the Ainur, the harmony of the archetypes. But Eä, the 'World that Is' begins, as in the Book of Genesis, with Word and with Light.

Tolkien's Tree of Tales grew from a single seed. In one of his letters he describes the exact moment when that seed began to burst with life. In 1913 he happened to be reading a poem called Crist by the eighth-century Anglo-Saxon writer Cynewulf, when he was struck by a single haunting verse (in translation as follows):

> Hail Earendel, brightest of Angels,
> Over Middle-Earth sent unto men.

'I felt a curious thrill,' he wrote, 'as if something had stirred in me, half wakened from sleep. There was something very remote and strange and beautiful behind those words, if I could grasp it, far beyond the ancient English.'

Over the years, 'Earendel', now 'Eärendil', became for Tolkien the great ancestor of the kings of Númenor, messenger of the Two Kindreds to the Lords of the West. To obtain their help to defeat the great Enemy, Morgoth (of whom Sauron is but a servant), he had to set foot upon the forbidden beaches of Eldamar. Unable thereafter to return to the Middle-earth he had saved, the Valar set him in the skies to voyage forever as the Morning Star. Shining upon his brow was a Silmaril, last of the three jewels made by Fëanor in the far past, filled with the light that had long since perished from the world. In this way the verse of Cynewulf had grown into a whole mythology:

> Hail Eärendil,
> bearer of light before the Sun and Moon!
> Splendour of the Children of Earth,
> star in the darkness,
> jewel in the sunset,
> radiant in the morning!

But how did the Silmaril *come* to Eärendil? It was this question that led Tolkien to Beren and Lúthien, at the very core of the mythological system of which *The Lord of the Rings* is merely a fragment, and at the centre of his conception of heroism.

It is told in *The Silmarillion* how in the First Age of the world, Beren, a mortal man, falls in love with Lúthien, the 'most beautiful of all the children of Ilúvatar', immortal daughter of Thingol, Elf-King of Doriath, when he catches sight of her dancing in the moonlight. Finding his way to Doriath through many perils, he asks her hand in marriage. To get rid of this unwelcome and unworthy suitor, King Thingol decides to send him on an impossible Quest. Long ago, Morgoth, the Great Enemy, had stolen from the uttermost West the three Silmarils – the most precious of all jewels. The Silmarils had been made to house light from the beginning of the world, a living light more ancient than the sun and moon. Proclaiming himself King of the World, Morgoth embedded the Silmarils in a great Iron Crown and placed it on his own head. 'His hands were burned black by the touch of those hallowed jewels, and black they remained ever after; nor was he ever free from the pain of the burning, and the anger of the pain. That crown he never took from his head, though its weight became a deadly weariness.' The jewels, therefore, were treasured in the fortress of evil itself above all wealth, 'and Balrogs [spirits of flame] were about them, and countless swords, and strong bars, and unassailable walls, and the dark majesty of Morgoth'.

Thingol will accede to Beren's request only if he brings him a Silmaril from Morgoth's crown. Well aware that the King intends the challenge as a sentence of death, Beren laughs. 'For little price do Elven-kings sell their daughters: for gems, and things made by craft. But if this be your will, Thingol, I will perform it. And when we meet again my hand shall hold a Silmaril from the Iron Crown.' How he achieves this Quest is a long story about light and darkness and human love, which I will briefly summarize. On his way to recover the holy jewel, Beren is soon cast into a pit to be devoured by werewolves. Lúthien, however, has followed after him (contrary to every stereotype of passive womanhood) and rescues him with the aid of her ancestral magic and with the friendship of Huan, the hound of the gods. They achieve the Quest together: it is she who captivates Morgoth and puts him to sleep while Beren cuts loose the Silmaril. They escape from Angband only to be confronted at the Gate by its most dreadful guardian: the monstrous wolf Carcharoth (the 'Red Maw'), named also Anfauglir, the 'Jaws of Thirst'. Thinking the light of the Silmaril will daunt the beast, Beren holds it aloft, but Carcharoth bites off his hand at the wrist. The Silmaril burns its way through the guts of the wolf, and drives him away in a tormented fury.

Rescued from the wrath of Morgoth by eagles, Beren returns to Thingol to claim his bride. 'What of your quest, and of your vow?' asks the King. Beren replies simply, 'It is fulfilled. Even now a Silmaril is in my hand,' and slowly raises the empty stump. Thingol relents, but before long the Wolf attacks the Hidden Kingdom of the Elves, and Beren understands that the Quest must continue. Together with Thingol he rides out for the final hunt. They meet Carcharoth, Huan is slain, and Beren is mortally wounded defending Thingol. The tale continues, however. Like Ishtar or Orpheus, Lúthien follows Beren to the underworld of the dead, and appeals over the head of Death himself to the Lord of the Valar to make an exception to the normal rules that separate the destinies of Men and Elves. She rejects the fate of the Elves, which is reincarnation, in favour of a human death in order to be with Beren for ever. The couple are rewarded with a brief return to life in Middle-earth, before their final journey into the unknown. From their marriage comes Thingol's heir Dior, then Eärendil's wife Elwing, the mother of Elrond and also of the line of Númenorean kings leading to Aragorn. Through Dior passes the Silmaril, until it arrives with Elwing and Eärendil. In a later Age of the world, it is a beam of light from this same Silmaril, captured in a crystal phial, that Galadriel gives Frodo as a comfort and protection on his journey into Mordor.

The tale of Beren and Lúthien is retold by Bilbo to Frodo, and by the Elves at Rivendell, and is recalled by the characters at many points in *The Lord of the Rings*. The love story of Aragorn and Arwen (narrated in the Appendices to *The Lord of the Rings*) is clearly modelled upon it. It clearly helps the protagonists to understand their own mission, just as it helped Tolkien to understand his own. The two worlds come together in death: a gravestone in the Catholic cemetery at Wolvercote identifies the author with Beren and Edith with Lúthien. *Light must be recovered from darkness, even at the cost of life itself, if we are to become worthy of love.* The will of man cannot aspire without sin to the 'Imperishable Flame' that is the eternal source of being. But, as in the Silmarils of Fëanor, human creativity can fashion a place on earth for that light to shine, recalling or prolonging the lost perfection of innocence, and contributing to the final perfection of a time-beyond-time to come. The war waged by evil to gain possession of the light seems unending, but in the midst of tragedy hope never dies.

Lúthien descends like Ishtar to rescue her consort from death. She enchants the god of the underworld with music like Orpheus. But her role in Tolkien's story can be understood best from a Christian perspective once it is realized that her beauty and her descent from the gods (her mother is one of the divine race of Maiar) enable her to function as a pure symbol of divine grace. She follows after Beren in much the same way as the divine assistance which comes to us at crucial moments in our own individual Quests. Without the help of grace we could achieve nothing: like Beren, we are soon thrown into the pit of despair to be devoured by were-wolves. We lack both the power and the freedom of action to achieve what we have promised to God and our own hearts.

In his love, God follows after us to supply whatever we lack, provided only we have done the best we can on our own. This is supremely true when we come to the moment of death ('pray for us sinners now and at the hour of our death', the Catholic implores the Blessed Virgin Mary).

Beren must lose his hand before Lúthien can put hers in its place. That is the way grace works: our own hand, our own ability to grasp and act, can only take us so far. In reality as in story, life itself must be renounced, every sacrifice accepted, for the sake of love, before love can finally conquer even death, and man be united with grace beyond the grave. Of this final destiny, the return of Beren and Lúthien after death to Tol Galen ('the Green Isle') and the birth to them of Dior the Beautiful, are symbols. In time they died once more, although 'none marked where at last their bodies lay'.

Through the power of his mythic imagination, Tolkien evoked the tragedy and the mystery of death against the backdrop of an even greater mystery: that of existence itself. The sense of loss, of a world passing away, fills his books like the sound of the sea and the glimmer of starlight; but for there to be loss, there must first have been possession. The destruction of the Trees that gave light before the Sun and Moon, the successive falls of Menegroth, Nargothrond, Gondolin and Númenor, leading to the removal or 'hiding' of Valinor (the Paradise of the West), add layer upon layer to the mood of nostalgia for a vanished Golden Age. As in all the great mythological systems of the world, each cycle of restoration ends with a fall. The Elves are immortal nature spirits bound to the world through reincarnation, and so their existence is permeated by this sense of tragedy. 'For now the Kindler, Varda, the Queen of the Stars, from Mount Everwhite has uplifted her hands like clouds, and all paths are drowned deep in shadow; and out of a grey country darkness lies on the foaming waves between us, and mist covers the jewels of Calacirya for ever.' The Elves can hope for nothing higher than memory: a frozen image of perfect beauty in the Far West.

If Tolkien had not been a Christian, perhaps this would have been something like his final word. But Men are not Elves, and the hope of Men transcends time. 'In sorrow we must go, but not in despair. Behold! we are not bound for ever to the circles of the world, and beyond them is more than memory.' These are the last words of Aragorn, King Elessar, to Queen Arwen. The death of man involves a definitive departure from this world into an unknown future. When it becomes a choice – as it is for Arwen, who, like Lúthien before her, chooses not to be counted among the Elves but to grow old and die – it is an act of faith in the Maker of all things, and in the love he has placed within the human heart. In the end, through both life and death only Ilúvatar the Creator can triumph over Morgoth, whose will determines the tragedy of the Fall. This he will do, *The Silmarillion* hints, not by forcing the free will of his creatures, but by weaving their own failures and sins into a yet greater design of his own. Morgoth will then perceive that his pride has made him an 'instrument in the devising of things more wonderful, which he himself hath not imagined'.

We come at last to *The Lord of the Rings* itself – in which Tolkien builds a bridge from the imaginal landscapes of his Northern 'Dreamtime' to our own Age, the Age of Men. *The Lord of the Rings* begins and ends in the 'Shire', a pure archetype of the semi-rural England that Tolkien loved, still recognizable in parts of Oxfordshire. (Buckland is, after all, only a half-hour's drive from The Broad.) The Quest it describes is, on the surface of things, a quest not to find a treasure but to lose one. The ring of invisibility acquired by Bilbo Baggins from Gollum in *The Hobbit* is discovered to be the long-lost Ring of Power forged by the Dark Lord, greatest servant of Morgoth (himself now exiled from the world), in the fires of Mount Doom. It will inevitably corrupt the wearer, or return to its maker, enabling him to conquer Middle-earth, unless it is unmade in the place of its creation. As Bilbo's heir, Frodo undertakes the Quest, supported by his servant Sam and friends Merry and Pippin. In a sense, then, the Quest to destroy the Ring before it is captured by the Enemy *is*, after all, a Quest *for* treasure: the treasure in this case being not the Ring itself but lasting security for the idyll of the Shire, Tolkien's idyll, which we find is already compassed about with danger and threatened by corruption from within. The application to our own late twentieth-century predicament is brought out by the fact that Tolkien describes the moral corruption eating away at the Shire as having a very clear physical expression: smokestacks, pollution and deforestation – in fact all the paraphernalia of industrial modernity. (On this theme see Patrick Curry's *Defending Middle-Earth: Tolkien, Myth and Modernity*: Floris, Edinburgh, 1997.) *The Lord of the Rings* therefore reaches two distinct climaxes. The first of these is the destruction of the Dark Lord in Mordor and the coronation of Aragorn as King Elessar in Gondor. The second climax, however, is in a way more important: Tolkien calls it the 'scouring of the Shire'. We could perhaps call it the 'scouring of Oxfordshire', a task that in our world must await the heroes of a new millennium.

The richness of the book's texture (a richness that makes it more like real life) is enhanced by the fact that it has many heroes. Each of the main characters has his own personal Quest, and Tolkien interweaves all these destinies in something of the way different lives are woven together in the real world. Frodo, of course, is the main protagonist and 'Ringbearer', the one to whom the White Council entrusts the mission to destroy the Ring. The man Strider is at first merely a mysterious outsider, a guide and companion for the Hobbits, but emerges as true hero by winning the throne of the two kingdoms of Middle-earth along with the hand of his Elven princess. The third main hero is the wizard Gandalf, leader of the nine Companions of the Ring and co-ordinator of the campaign against the Dark Lord throughout Middle-earth.

Even more clearly than in *The Silmarillion*, heroism in *The Lord of the Rings* takes an unmistakably Christian form. Each of the three main heroes I have mentioned is a kind of 'Christ-figure'. Each offers his life for others, each passes through darkness and even a kind of death to a kind of resurrection. Gandalf defends the Companions against the demonic Balrog on the narrow bridge of Moria, and falls with his enemy into the fiery pit. Victorious in death, he is eventually 'sent back', no longer as Gandalf the Grey, but endowed with even greater authority and power as Gandalf the White. Strider/Aragorn also 'harrows hell' by daring the Paths of the Dead under the haunted mountain, and summons the spirits of the dead oathbreakers to his side at the black stone of Erech. Finally, Frodo passes through Shelob's impenetrable darkness under Minas Morgul, through an unconsciousness that Sam cannot distinguish from death, into the Land of Shadow itself. But in his case, identification with the suffering Christ continues even after the victory achieved by so many sacrifices. His wounds, through which he becomes increasingly 'full of light', can never entirely be healed in Middle-earth. From the Grey Havens he passes into the West, his departure with the great Elves and Gandalf marking the end of the Third Age of the world.

The book, however, does not end even with Frodo's departure. It ends with Sam returning from the Havens and sitting down with his baby daughter in his lap. This brings us to the fourth and – I would argue – central hero of *The Lord of the Rings*: Samwise Gamgee. For it is Sam, more than Frodo, who is the incarnation of the Shire, and most deeply rooted in its soil. In *The Lord of the Rings*, Sam's growing to maturity and the healing of the Shire go hand in hand. This makes perfect sense, for, as Tolkien once wrote (*Letters*, p. 181), the plot is concerned with 'the ennoblement (or sanctification) of the humble'. *The Lord of the Rings* is a story in which 'the first will be last and the last will be first'. The Hobbits are humble, and Sam is the humblest of Hobbits, a servant without pretensions or ambitions – except perhaps to have a garden of his own. For him to leave the Shire out of love for his master Frodo involves a great sacrifice. In a sense, he has to sacrifice the Shire itself – consciously when he sees the threat to the Shire in Galadriel's Mirror but still determines to go on. It is fidelity to Frodo that remains his guiding star throughout. The plans of the Wise and the fate of Middle-earth are never his concern. He only knows he has to do his bit and help his master, however hopeless the task may seem. At a crucial moment in Mordor he must carry the Ringbearer and even the Ring itself. He moves from immature to mature innocence; and finally, back in his own sphere (which is Tolkien's own inner world of the Shire) the gardener and healer of gardens becomes a 'king' – or at least a Mayor. In fact, the Appendices tell us that he was elected Mayor of the Shire no less than seven times, and it is to him that King Elessar will in the end entrust the Star of the Dúnedain, representing the crown of the North Kingdom.

To read *The Lord of the Rings* as, in a special way, Sam's story, makes it even more our story. The great events of the book begin as well as end with Sam. A self-professed lover of tales about Elves and dragons, caught by Gandalf eavesdropping under Frodo's window at Bag End, Sam is hauled in by the ears and becomes part of the action from that moment on. In all of this, he represents you and me, the reader. Like him, we love stories about Elves. We too are 'caught by the ears' and yanked over the threshold into the world of the Quest, a Quest that promises the transformation of the mundane into the magical.

Transformation, however, comes at a price. Evil must be faced and overcome. Gollum, despised and outcast, represents the weakness and evil that lurks in the soul of a Hobbit – even of a Hobbit like Sam. In Jungian terms, Gollum is Sam's (and Frodo's) Shadow. Sam frequently advises Frodo to kill him when he has the chance. The hatred between them is one of the themes of their journey into the Land of Shadow itself. On some level there is a connection between the vulnerability of Sam to that hatred for a Hobbit long ago corrupted by the Ring and the evident vulnerability of the Shire to the corruption of modernity, the corruption brought upon it by Saruman during the War of the Ring. Hobbiton can only be healed by the reordering of the Hobbit soul; and Sam's soul is only reordered and healed at the very end of the Quest, on the side of Mount Doom, by first sparing and finally forgiving Gollum.

The Ring is a symbol of pride and power. It represents everything that draws us into the kingdom of the Dark Lord by tempting us to become like him. Its circular shape is that of the will closed upon itself. Its empty centre suggests the void into which we thrust ourselves by using the Ring. The invisibility with which it cloaks the wearer at the same time severs our normal relationships with those around us. We all have such a Ring: it forms the foundations of our own Dark Tower, namely the Ego, the false self. Our Quest, like Frodo's and Sam's, is to renounce the Ring and be rid of the hold it has over us, ultimately on the path that only Christ has travelled to the end: by sacrificing himself for his friends. If this is what the Ring means, its renunciation is impossible, as Tolkien saw, without help from 'outside', from beyond ourselves. (In theology this is called grace.) The self cannot unmake the self. 'I can will what is right, but I cannot do it,' as St Paul says (Romans 7:18–19). On the very brink of success, Frodo's free will having taken him as far as it can, the Ringbearer dramatically renounces the Quest and claims the Ring for his own. His freedom to cast it away has been eroded by the task of bearing it to Mount Doom. What finally saves him is an apparent accident, which is in fact the direct consequence of his own earlier (and freer) decision to spare the life of Gollum. That was an act of pure compassion. Thus in a way it is not Frodo who saves Middle-earth at all. Even less is it Gollum, who bites the Ring from his hand and in so doing falls into the Fire. It is not even Sam, who has learned compassion from Frodo, and without whom Frodo would never have reached Mount Doom. The Saviour of Middle-earth turns out to be One who works through the love and freedom of his creatures, and who forgives us our trespasses 'as we forgive those who trespass against us' (*Letters*, p. 181), using even our mistakes and the designs of the Enemy (as already hinted in *The Silmarillion*) to bring about our good. The ending of *The Lord of the Rings* is a triumph of Providence over Fate, but it is also a triumph of Mercy, in which free will, supported by grace, is fully vindicated.

The Quest achieved, waiting to be engulfed in the ruin of Mount Doom, Sam sighs to Frodo, 'What a tale we have been in, Mr Frodo, haven't we? I wish I could hear it told! Do you think they'll say: *Now comes the story of Nine-Fingered Frodo and the Ring of Doom*? And then everyone will hush, like we did, when in Rivendell they told us the tale of Beren One-Hand and the Great Jewel. I wish I could hear it! And I wonder how it will go on after our part.' To the reader, Frodo and Sam are characters in a story; to Frodo and Sam, their adventures are real life and the world of 'story' lies elsewhere – in the ancient tales they have heard from Bilbo and the Elves. But in this crucial moment of insight, Sam has bridged the gap, and seen their own lives as part of a great tale full of wonder and meaning, that stretches from the beginning of time to its mysterious end. In the same moment, he overcomes the distance between himself and the reader of the tale of Frodo and the Ring of Doom. We live, not in another world, but in an extension of his.

Sam's significant reference to Beren One-Hand is reinforced by a slightly earlier remark of his on Mount Doom, immediately after Gollum falls into the Fire. 'The burden was gone.

His master had been saved; he was himself again, he was free. And then Sam caught sight of the maimed and bleeding hand. "Your poor hand!" he said. "And I have nothing to bind it with, or comfort it. I would have spared him a whole hand of mine rather. But he's gone now beyond recall, gone for ever."' The desire to grasp is finally renounced; the grasping Shadow falls into the Fire and is forgiven. Frodo has lost a finger, and humble Sam may see him as the great hero, but by that remark and the spirit it reveals it is Sam himself who is conformed to Beren One-Hand; Sam, not Frodo, whose touch will bring the Shire back to life in a new golden age.

The Fall of Man opened a chasm filled with fire between the real and the ideal; between truth and goodness. The bridge of beauty is damaged beyond repair, yet join the two sides we must, by making our own existence into a path across the Abyss for others: everyone who does so becomes both Hero and King. In the biblical book of Revelation we are told: 'To him who conquers I will give some of the hidden manna, and I will give him a white stone, with a new name written on the stone which no one knows except him who receives it' (2:17). This 'new name' is the eternal identity, the transfigured personality, the hidden treasure that each of us is here on earth to discover. But it is not a matter of discovery only, but one of making, of subcreation. God is waiting for the response of our freedom. Our own choice, our own creativity, is essential to the drama, and this makes the world a drama fraught with real peril.

Tolkien saw in the Christian revelation the meeting and fusing of Legend and History, and in the Body of Christ the restored bridge from this world to the other. All along our hearts spoke true. They were made for what they long to find; nature was made for grace. The Maker himself has once and for all vindicated those fleeting glimpses of 'Joy beyond the walls of the world, poignant as grief', which art affords us.

3

MODERNITY IN MIDDLE-EARTH
PATRICK CURRY

Patrick Curry was born in Winnipeg, Canada in 1951. He has lived in London for the last twenty-five years. He has a B.A., an M.Sc., and a Ph.D. from the University of London. He is now an independent scholar and writer. His books include A Confusion of Prophets: Victorian and Edwardian Astrology, Machiavelli for Beginners, *and* Defending Middle-Earth: Tolkien, Myth and Modernity.

The Lord of the Rings is a book that can be appreciated, and celebrated, in many different ways. In my study of it, *Defending Middle-Earth: Tolkien, Myth and Modernity*,[1] I concentrated on its contemporary meaning – what Tolkien called its 'applicability'[2] – in cultural, social and political terms. This is not to deny its other strengths: as a remarkable feat of narrative, as an extraordinary work of philology and linguistics, or as a deeply felt meditation on the meaning of human life when faced with inevitable death. But neither should these aspects obscure the first set of meanings, which Tolkien's hostility to literal-minded allegory, certainly correct in itself, has tended to obscure. In any case, it is highly simplistic to see his book in just one way, to the exclusion of others. If, for example, it is 'about Death and the desire for deathlessness' (in Tolkien's own words), can it not also be concerned with the drive for worldly 'Power and Domination'? Indeed, does this not suggest that the former may be the very motor of the latter?[3]

To this extent, as I have argued, Tolkien's work that has had the greatest public impact is an account of resistance to the contemporary threat to three great goods, nested one inside another. First there is community: the hobbits, social to the ends of their well-brushed toes, and firmly rooted in their place, the Shire. Next there is nature: Middle-earth itself in all its wonders, from talking trees (emphatically not tree-like humans) to malevolent mountains, encompassing not only the Shire but every other place and its related race. Then there are spiritual values: the Sea, which alone escapes the compass of Middle-earth, over which lies the *fons et origo* of its history and healing from its travails, something which the Ringbearers are finally granted. Where these dimensions overlap is the heart of Tolkien's tale. Finally, in stark contrast, the single-visioned, imperialist perfection of power that threatens the survival of these three – after whom *The Lord of the Rings* is named – is, of course, embodied in Sauron and Mordor.

It is also very much to the point that Tolkien's tale is set in an imaginary (distant) time, but its place is the 'mother-earth' that we all share.[4] And our Middle-earth, as Tolkien clearly perceived, is also in grave danger: communities steadily replaced by congeries of consumers; the natural support-systems of our own and other species (those that remain: the big mammals, like the great forests, are going fast) destroyed at an unprecedented and utterly unsustainable rate; and any ultimate values denied beyond the bread and circuses of instrumental knowledge, material consumption and sensational entertainment. This is the culmination of a process that began to show itself in the seventeenth century, achieved self-consciousness in the eighteenth, developed new forms and strength in the nineteenth, and continues ever more powerfully (if still unevenly) in our own, under the banner of economic globalization. My shorthand term for it is 'modernity', but it has at least three main strands which can be distinguished (but not separated), all of which Tolkien's work calls into fundamental question: the nation-state, science and technology, and financial capital. Thus, insofar as *The Lord of the Rings* is about this world, we find ourselves reading an account of how, beyond foretelling, it was saved from the final triumph of this power.

The overwhelming reception of such an otherwise utterly unlikely book – around fifty million copies sold worldwide, to date, in at least thirty languages – is evidence, I think, that Tolkien's insights, fears and hopes in relation to modernity strike a profound chord with the reading public. Indeed, in addition to its affinities with 'human nature', what has made his book, with its local, even parochial roots, an effectively universal literary phenomenon, is precisely the global extent of the crisis it addresses.

Of course, the other aspect of that phenomenon is the incomprehension and/or visceral hostility of most of its professional literary critics.[5] But this simply confirms my explanation. Of course, just as *The Lord of the Rings* has more than one aspect or dimension, it is quite possible to dislike it for different reasons: on grounds of literary taste, for example, or religious or philosophical disagreement. But the dominant charge against Tolkien has been that of escapism and/or reaction; and the overwhelming majority of these critics, as is evident from their other writings, subscribe to the very same values of modernity – statism, scientism, economism and secularism – which are implicated in the pathological dynamic that so alarmed Tolkien, and still deeply worries his readers today. However inchoately, they perceive the cultural nihilism, social upheaval and ecological destruction that the ideology of Progress tries to disguise; and however mixed their feelings about it, they are not fooled, whereas the educated elite of *clercs* is, by and large, because they have conveniently fooled themselves. As Tolkien memorably put it, they confuse, 'not always by sincere error, the Escape of the Prisoner with the Flight of the Deserter'.[6] And for whom is 'escapism' such a crime? For the jailers, naturally, of whatever kind.

The term commonly associated with 'escapism' is, of course, 'fantasy'. But the irony here becomes apparent when we ask who exactly is indulging in fantasy: those who, like Tolkien, find community, nature and the spirit worth fighting for (and as do the protagonists in *The Lord of the Rings*, literally); or those who claim that science is the only legitimate kind of knowledge, that economic growth can continue forever, that nature can sustain whatever we do to her – and that we have a right to do to her whatever we want?

Tolkien deserves credit for having perceived the destructive consequences of modernity long before the great majority of his peers, and his fears have been strikingly confirmed; while the Panglossian promises of the modernists, humanists and technocrats – including their literary apologists – are repeatedly deferred, never to be realized. Perhaps his prescience is not altogether surprising. As a conservative Catholic medievalist, he was sufficiently marginal to the mainstream to see the modern world relatively objectively, yet sufficiently erudite to contextualize and articulate his perceptions (and creative, to embody them artistically). Yet he also deserves acclaim for his courage in swimming against such a powerful tide.

What is the situation now? Tolkien once remarked (in 1959) that 'I look East, West, North, South, and I do not see Sauron; but I see that Saruman has many descendents.'[7] Let us pay him the compliment of taking him at his word. After the main events of the War of the Ring, Saruman still managed to inflict great damage on the Shire: a kind of damage we are indeed all too familiar with today as 'development'. It is an institutionalization of the relentless drive for short-term profit for a powerful few. And like the activities of Sharkey, its effects are socially divisive and fragmenting, ecologically destructive, and in all senses unsustainable. True, it is not Mordor triumphant, not the more direct infliction of evil (or the infliction of more open evil) of this century, such as in the heydays of Nazism, Stalinism and Maoism. But in the not-so-long term, if unchecked, the results will converge. As various references in *The Lord of the Rings* point out, Saruman was still doing Mordor's work, even after the passing of Sauron.

It is hard to see how global modernization could be checked, let alone halted – without, at least, a cure at least as terrible as the disease. Yet Tolkien's moral legacy is not despair, but hope; as Gandalf rightly says, 'despair is only for those who see the end beyond all doubt. We do not.'[8] Like Frodo, Sam and the rest of the Company, our duty is plain: not to give up, but do what we each can for the things, places and people (non-human as well) that we know and love. And although Tolkien was careful to specify that such hope is 'without guarantees'[9] – including, I would add, religious or even specifically Christian ones – the success of the Ringbearer's mission does, I think, give people hope that we too may win through, and live to wake up in a world of relative security, peace and dignity. Far from encouraging quietism, such hope enables and encourages people to act. It forms a virtuous circle, I think, with two other aspects of Tolkien's work: the love of, and power of, place; and the value of sheer wonder.[10] Taken together, for those who are not already too far gone, his mythopoeic fiction can fulfil one of the chief virtues of the myths and fairytales which are its literary forebears: recovery.[11]

This would be remarkable enough. But *The Lord of the Rings* is still, in a profound way, about inevitable loss, and the passing away – simply with time, but specifically with the passing of the three Elven rings – of many fair things. So even recovery from evils that can be remedied, and the unnecessary sadness they cause, only opens on to the existential reality of life, and death. But here the worldly interpretation of the book that I have emphasized again finds its place, without contradiction, in relation to a 'deeper' or more personal meaning. For as Gandalf says, 'not all tears are an evil'; such sadness can be 'blessed and without bitterness'.[12] This maturity is the final glory of a legacy all too rare in contemporary literature, and one indeed to celebrate.

NOTES

1. Edinburgh: Floris, 1997 and New York: St. Martin's Press, 1998.

2. J. R. R. Tolkien, *The Lord of the Rings*, London: HarperCollins, 1995, p. xvii.

3. Humphrey Carpenter (ed.), *The Letters of J. R. R. Tolkien*, London: Allen & Unwin, 1981, p. 203.

4. Carpenter, *The Letters of J. R. R. Tolkien*, p. 283.

5. See my 'Tolkien and his Critics: A Critique', forthcoming in Thomas Honegger and Peter Buchs (eds.), *Root and Branch: Approaches towards Understanding Tolkien*, Zurich & Berne: Walking Tree Books, 1999.

6. J. R. R. Tolkien, 'On Fairy Stories', pp. 9–74 (p. 56) in *Tree and Leaf*, London: Allen & Unwin, 1988; since republished by Harper-Collins.

7. Patricia Reynolds and Glen H. Good-Knight (eds.), *Proceedings of the J. R. R. Tolkien Centenary Conference*, Milton Keynes: The Tolkien Society, and Altadena: The Mythopoeic Press, 1995, pp. 307–8; cf. Tolkien, *Letters*, p. 235.

8. Tolkien, *The Lord of the Rings*, p. 262.

9. Carpenter, *The Letters of J. R. R. Tolkien*, p. 237.

10. See my *Defending Middle-Earth*, chapter 6.

11. See Tolkien, 'On Fairy Stories'.

12. Tolkien, *The Lord of the Rings*, pp. 1006–7.

4

J. R. R. Tolkien and the Art of the Parable
Robert Murray SJ

Father Murray was a close personal friend of Tolkien and from 1944, when his intimacy with the Tolkien family began, Tolkien handed him drafts of The Lord of the Rings *to read in manuscript and proof. The extent to which his critical judgement was respected can be gauged from Tolkien's belief that Father Murray was 'more perceptive, especially in some directions, than anyone else'. The following is Father Murray's sermon preached at the Thanksgiving service at the 1992 Tolkien Centenary Conference in Oxford.*

With many such parables he spoke the word to them, as they were able to hear it; he did not speak to them without a parable.
(Mark 4:33–34)

I do not know of Tolkien's ever being asked to preach a sermon, but he had a high ideal of what a good sermon should be.

Good sermons require some art, some virtue, some knowledge. Real sermons require some special grace which does not transcend art but arrives at it by instinct or 'inspiration'; indeed the Holy Spirit seems sometimes to speak through a human mouth providing art, virtue and insight he does not himself possess: but the occasions are rare.[1]

Tolkien recognized this gift in his parish priest, Douglas Carter, one of whose sermons inspired a long and theologically rich letter to his son Christopher.[2] That was in October 1944, just about the time that I, newly arrived in Oxford, was discovering the joy of friendship with the Tolkiens. Less than eighteen months later, when they realized that I was being drawn to share their faith, they introduced me to Father Carter, which led to a lasting friendship with that wonderful man and preacher.

But sermons should not be overburdened with reminiscences; and Tolkien, though he enjoyed being honoured, would not have wanted a sermon to be focused on him, but only on the things of God. Yet it seemed right to choose a text on which we can usefully bring some of Tolkien's ideas to bear. As far as I know, he left few if any writings directly on the Bible; yet if we consider the text I have chosen, about how Jesus taught through parables, we can find in Tolkien's writings not only many passages bearing on the nature and power of this art in which Jesus excelled, but also wonderful examples of the art itself, though Tolkien never claimed the term 'parable' for any of his own stories.

'With many such parables,' says Mark, '[Jesus] spoke the word to them, as they were able to hear it.' In this sentence, clearly, 'the word' stands for what Jesus intended to communicate, while 'parables' are the means which he adopted. 'The word', of course, means the Gospel, the Good News. As for 'parable', today it is probably often thought of as a kind of story implying a meaning, but this is rather *allegory*, which is only one of the many verbal arts covered by the biblical terms (Hebrew and Greek) which we translate by 'parable'. The primary sense is 'comparison', but also included are allegory, proverb, satire and almost any verbal image, metaphor or paradoxical saying. Starting from the modern sense we might wonder if it is true that Jesus never taught except in parables; but if we realize that the term includes all his vivid images – 'the lilies of the field [which] neither toil nor spin', or 'blind guides' – then the statement is seen to be more broadly true.

Mark says that Jesus spoke the Word to the people 'as they were able to hear it', implying that he chose the medium of parable so as to temper his message to their capacity. But the question can be looked at in two ways: parable can be viewed in its attractive and stimulating power, or in its comparative obscurity as a mode of communication. The evangelists take the second viewpoint, and connect Jesus' use of parable with the fact which deeply troubled them, as it did Paul, namely that a large proportion of the Jews had not accepted Jesus as the Messiah and his teaching as the Word of God. Today, however, I would like to consider Jesus' parables rather in their art, as the method chosen by a wonderful teacher.

Mark's phrase 'as they were able to hear it', though only a brief hint, is relevant to both aspects of the question why Jesus used parables. Mark implies that Jesus took account of the capacity of his audiences, realizing how they varied both in education and in openness to him; he therefore chose not to confront them all immediately with a challenge for which many might not be ready, but rather to use a medium which could first attract and then fascinate and tease the mind, even for a long time, till the hearers might form their own response.

Parable, in its biblical range of meaning, is a skilful use of the arts of speech so as not to impose or compel, but to invite a response in which the hearer is personally active. One of the most instructive examples in the Bible is the parable by which the prophet Nathan brought David to repentance for his adultery and virtual murder (2 Samuel 12). He tells the king a touching little story of a powerful rich man who forced a poor man to give up his one beloved ewe lamb. David erupts with a rage which betrays his inward turmoil, for his reaction is out of proportion to the circumstances in the story, but much more appropriate to his own sin. In itself the parable expressed no personal accusation; yet it so played on David's imagination and feelings that it awakened his benumbed conscience and prepared him to discover and face the truth about himself. Only when the parable had done its work did Nathan turn the naked light of reality on David: 'You are the man ...' Since then, for every reader, this whole episode in the story of David has itself become a parable – for the power of stories to act as parables depends not on whether they are fictitious or factually true, but on whether they possess that potential universality which makes others find them applicable, through an imaginative perception of analogy, to other situations.

At this point you will all have picked up one of Tolkien's memorable words, 'applicable'. He used it often when discussing the power of stories to suggest more to the reader than they say, without their being artificial allegories. He always insisted, of course, on the autonomy of story as an art in itself, which needs no other justification than to arouse delight. A good story need not have a 'message', yet Tolkien often acknowledged that most great stories, whether as wholes or in many particulars, abound in morally significant features which are applicable to the experience of readers far removed in time and place from the storyteller. In other words (though I do not think he ever said so), many stories partake of the nature of parable. There is, however, one species within the genus parable which Tolkien did discuss explicitly, and with an ambivalent attitude to it, namely allegory. He often expressed dislike of it, both in general and in C. S. Lewis's use of it. In his Foreword to *The Lord of the Rings* he said about allegory:

> I much prefer history, true or feigned, with its varied
> applicability to the thought and experience of readers. I
> think that many confuse 'applicability' with 'allegory';

but the one resides in the freedom of the reader, and the other in the purposed domination of the author.[3]

Tolkien could not, however, refuse allegory some place, provided it were kept in it. It could serve in an argument; there he was quite prepared to make up allegories and call them such, as he did twice in two pages of his great lecture on *Beowulf*.[4] But even when discussing story he could be more tolerant of allegory, and allow that

> any attempt to explain the purport of myth or fairytale must use allegorical language. (And, of course, the more 'life' a story has the more readily will it be susceptible of allegorical interpretations: while the better a deliberate allegory is made the more nearly will it be acceptable just as a story.)[5]

All this is relevant to the interpretation of Jesus' parables, for it has long been a critical dogma that none of them is an allegory or may legitimately be interpreted as one. Yet allegory was part of the biblical parable genre; the prophetic books contain many examples, especially as a way of meditating on the history of Israel and other nations. Must Jesus be protected from the imputation that he ever told a story as an allegory, or that this may be among the possible modes of 'applicability'? Let us look at an example or two.

Matthew, Mark and Luke all begin their presentation of Jesus' parables with the Sower. This starts with a simple picture from ordinary life. It could have remained just that, a natural symbol, the potency of which to produce metaphor Jesus might have released poetically by a few hints. But he goes on, describing the kinds of place where the seed might fall and its fate in each, ranging from frustrated germination to the greatest fruitfulness. There Jesus stops, with his habitual call: 'He who has ears to hear, let him hear.' (Even this is a metaphor, for physical hearing has ended; 'hearing' now means inward perception and response.)

Now the disciples ask for an explanation. (Here the evangelists insert their discussion about why Jesus' teaching was not accepted by so many of his own people.) The interpretation which is then presented as Jesus' own is fully allegorical, in terms of different human responses to the Word. Now modern scholars are almost all agreed that this comes from early Christian reflection, not from Jesus. They may well be right in their linguistic arguments; but if an interpretation is given in the words of a hearer, that need not mean that he misunderstood the speaker's drift or imposed his own ideas. What shall we conclude? It is clear that Jesus left the people with an open-ended picture of seed sown with various results; but he and his audience shared a tradition of teaching through images, and he was a preacher proclaiming a radical message about God of which many of them must have heard rumours. They could hardly fail to see in the sower an image of Jesus himself.

As for the meaning of the rest, he left them free, but he had baited a whole string of hooks. Allegory is woven into the fabric of the parable, but with a delicacy which does not spoil the joy of working it out for oneself. And for *that* reason I believe that the interpretation which is given is not precisely from Jesus. Not that it says what he did not mean, but that it says less than he may have meant. It focuses the application on many kinds of hearers in their various situations. But the parable can be applied by *an individual* to his or her varying situations and states. On another occasion Luke tells us that, when Jesus was picturing some scenes of servants behaving responsibly or not during their master's absence, Peter asked him: 'Lord, are you telling this parable for us or for all?' (Luke 12:41). A perceptive question; but Jesus answered only by another question, still within the imagery of his parable, which could lead Peter and every reader to realize that the answer is 'both'.

Tolkien's 'applicability' is a better, because more flexible, key to understanding Jesus' parables than any rigidly defined set of categories. Let us look at the Good Samaritan. In its context the story is spoken to help an inquirer, who has shown good will, to answer his own question 'who is my neighbour?' Jesus provocatively pictures a most hated kind of neighbour who does a most truly neighbourly action. The inquirer is forced to realize this. But then Jesus turns the question round: it is now no longer 'how should I define (that is, limit) the category of neighbour?', but 'how should I behave, now that I have had to recognize that *anyone* can be my neighbour?' Now in its own context this is a story which seems to function not allegorically, but by virtue of what each character actually does or suffers. It is an invented story, not history, but it could have happened. Each character is significant in himself, not by symbolizing someone else. What the story suggests is applicable to many other situations, but by the force of the good and bad examples it contains, not by allegory.

And yet it has been read allegorically. The church fathers developed an interpretation which makes the whole story and every detail into an allegory of the drama of sin and redemption. To give only some main points, 'he fell among robbers' refers to the Fall caused by Satan. The priest and the Levite represent the Jewish law as viewed by Paul. The Samaritan, interpreted as meaning 'guardian', symbolizes Christ; his mount, the incarnation; the inn is the Church, and so on. The whole thing is amazingly ingenious; it edified generations of Christians. But beside a straightforward reading of the parable in its own context, it seems simply perverse. And yet ... ? Is there not something about the Samaritan's compassion and taking trouble which almost irresistibly makes a Christian reader think of Jesus? This thought can then easily lead the reader to identify with the wounded man, and then to universalize him. And there you have the germ of a reading which is allegorical. In fact we find a simple form of this kind within a century after Luke.[6] Is *this* perverse, or is it another possible aspect of the story's 'applicability'?

Once again I cannot do better than quote Tolkien:

> Of course, Allegory and Story converge, meeting somewhere in Truth. So that the only perfectly consistent allegory is a real life; and the only fully intelligible story is an allegory. And one finds, even in imperfect human 'literature', that the better and more consistent an allegory is the more easily can it be read 'just as a story'; and the better and more closely woven a story is the more easily can those so minded find allegory in it. But the two start out from opposite ends.[7]

'From opposite ends.' This exactly expresses the difference between, on the one hand, the development of natural symbolism by metaphor, simile or parable and, on the other, the artificiality of allegory. The one starts from things and human life in the actual world, seeing them as charged with natural symbolic potency; a flash of imaginative insight perceives how this potency can engender new meaning in another context, and so *meta-phora* occurs, the transference of a symbol's power so as to illuminate something else; but it is offered freely to whoever can respond. Jesus' greatest parables work as complex forms of this way of 'sub-creation', which we might call 'nature-based'; and so, of course, do Tolkien's own stories – though we must note that the material on which his imagination worked was as much human languages and words as the world and nature.

On the other side is allegory (of which poetic riddles may be regarded as singular specimens). The functioning of allegory is powered not so much by the symbolic potency latent in things or in human life as by a plan or message which the author conceals under artificially constructed symbols, with clues to lead the reader to discover what is the intended solution in the actual world. All this, I believe, is implicit in those short phrases in which Tolkien says that story and allegory 'start out from opposite ends', and that the applicability of 'the one resides in the freedom of the reader, and the other in the purposed domination of the author'.[8] But it is also important that he recognized that, in the greatest stories and allegorical narratives, the qualities of both modes of sub-creation may overlap and mingle. And so they do in at least some of the parables of Jesus.

One more feature of Jesus' parables, and a very important one, is signally illuminated by Tolkien's literary insight. Many of the parables represent persons coming to a moment of decision, the outcome of which has all-important consequences. Undoubtedly Jesus intended, by picturing vivid examples, to confront people with a challenge to realize the reality of God in a new way, and to change their values and way of life. Everything would depend on how they took this turning-point. You can guess what, among Tolkien's ideas, I see as bearing on this feature of the parables: it is his focus on the climax and outcome to which a 'fairy-story' leads. In Greek literary theory this is called *katastrophe*, but to designate the diversity of outcomes, happy or unhappy, he coined the pair of terms *eucatastrophe* and *dyscatastrophe*. As a Christian, Tolkien saw 'the *eucatastrophic* tale' as 'the true form of fairy-tale, and its highest function'.[9] At this point the human sub-creative art of story becomes the 'far-off gleam or echo of *evangelium* in the real world',[10] the supreme Good News in human history. As well as in the essay 'On Fairy-Stories', Tolkien expressed this relationship powerfully in the poem 'Mythopoeia'.[11]

I will allude only briefly to examples of Tolkien's own 'sub-creation' which (though he would have been embarrassed by the suggestion) could be compared with biblical stories. The

Bible contains traces of various poetic creation myths besides the accounts in Genesis, especially in Job and the Psalms. But in all literatures since the formation of the sacred books of humankind surely there is hardly a creation myth to equal, in beauty and imaginative power, the one with which *The Silmarillion* begins. Here Tolkien projected his idea of sub-creation back to the beginning of all things, and conceived it in terms of music. Ilúvatar, the One, first created the Ainur, 'the Holy Ones, ... the offspring of his thought', and proposed themes for them to make music on. At last he called a halt, and then revealed that this music, both in its beauty and in the discords which had arisen within it, formed the archetypes and 'script' for a whole world and its history.[12]

I will say little here about *The Lord of the Rings*. Two of my quotations from Tolkien refer to his wish that it should not be read as an allegory. It is, of course, a monumental example of sub-creation of a Secondary World; its plot is woven with strands of *dyscatastrophe* and *eucatastrophe*. That he hoped that it could stand as 'a far-off gleam or echo of *evangelium*' is revealed in his published letter to myself, who had spoken of the concealed 'order of Grace',[13] and by the deep feeling of his reply to another correspondent, who had sensed in *The Lord of the Rings* 'a sanity and sanctity which is a power in itself'.[14] How could he have dreamed that, within thirty years of its publication, readers in Russia would be drawn to the Christian faith by reading it?

Two stories of Tolkien's, however, stand out as so rich in 'applicability' that it is not improper to call them parables, though entirely in the form of pure creations of fantasy: I mean, of course, *Leaf by Niggle* and *Smith of Wootton Major*. Both of them abound in those qualities of parable, of *eucatastrophe* and *evangelium*, which we have been considering. But we must remember the words of Roger Lancelyn Green about *Smith of Wootton Major* which pleased Tolkien: 'To seek for the meaning is to cut open the ball in search of its bounce.'[15] In place of comment, I would like to let play on these 'parables' of Tolkien some lines of poetry, though from a poet very unlike him. They are a stanza near the end of Browning's 'Abt Vogler': it is more exalted than the simplicity of *Leaf by Niggle*, but I think it says what the story hints at:

> All we have willed or hoped or dreamed of good shall exist;
>> Not its semblance, but itself; no beauty, nor good, nor power
> Whose voice has gone forth, but each survives for the melodist
>> When eternity affirms the conception of an hour.
> The high that proved too high, the heroic for earth too hard,
>> The passion that left the ground to lose itself in the sky,
> Are music sent up to God by the lover and the bard;
>> Enough that he heard it once: we shall hear it by-and-by.[16]

Tolkien held indeed that a product of creative fantasy could reflect a 'far-off gleam or echo of *evangelium*'. Could the world of 'Faerie', of which the humble Smith was secretly nothing less than king, even stand as a parable of the Kingdom preached by Jesus? Perhaps Tolkien was too conscious of the unbaptized roots of 'Faerie'. Yet here too poets, from Spenser to R. S. Thomas, can embolden us to take this step, and to call Tolkien, in his own way, a poet of the Kingdom.[17]

NOTES

1. Humphrey Carpenter (ed.), *The Letters of J. R. R. Tolkien*, London: Allen & Unwin, 1981, p. 75.

2. Ibid., pp. 99–102.

3. J. R. R. Tolkien, *The Lord of the Rings*, London: Allen & Unwin, one-volume edition, 1968, p. 11.

4. J. R. R. Tolkien, *The Monsters and the Critics and Other Essays*, London: Allen & Unwin, 1983, pp. 6–8.

5. Carpenter, *The Letters of J. R. R. Tolkien*, p. 145.

6. The simple allegorical hints come in Irenaeus, *Adv. Haer.* III, 17, 3. The complicated development was chiefly due to Origen (*Hom. On Luke* 34), and was summed up by Augustine (*Quaest. Evang.* II, 19). Cf. C. H. Dodd, *The Parables of the Kingdom*, London: Fontana Books, 1961, pp. 13–14.

7. Carpenter, *The Letters of J. R. R. Tolkien*, p. 121.

8. Cf. nn. 7 and 3.

9. J. R. R. Tolkien, *Tree and Leaf*, London: Allen & Unwin, 1988 edn., p. 62. Cf. also *Letters*, pp. 101–2. Tolkien's formations from the Greek *katastrophe* were a useful (as well as elegant) development because, whereas the Greek word was ambivalent, in English it has only a 'bad' sense.

10. Ibid., p. 64.

11. Ibid., pp. 97–101.

12. J. R. R. Tolkien, *The Silmarillion*, London: Allen & Unwin, 1977, pp. 15–22. Cf. *Letters*, p. 195: 'So in this myth, it is "feigned" (legitimately whether that is a feature of the real world or not) that He gave special "sub-creative" powers to certain of His highest created beings: that is a guarantee that what they devised and made should be given the reality of Creation.' Tolkien once told me that he liked to believe that God had given the angels some part in the work of creation. I took him to be expressing a theological speculation, since at that time I had not yet seen *The Silmarillion*.

13. Carpenter, *The Letters of J. R. R. Tolkien*, p. 172.

14. Ibid., p. 413.

15. Ibid., p. 388.

16. Robert Browning, *Dramatis Personae* (1864), 'Abt Vogler', stanza 10.

17. The sermon as delivered ended with a reading of R. S. Thomas's poem *The Kingdom* which was first published in Thomas's collection *H'm* (1972) and reprinted in *Later Poems: A Selection*, London: Macmillan, 1983, p. 35.

5

THE LORD OF THE RINGS – A CATHOLIC VIEW
CHARLES A. COULOMBE

Charles A. Coulombe was born in New York City on 8 November 1960. An avid Tolkien fan since he was thirteen, he delivered a paper at the 1992 Tolkien Centennial Conference at Keble College, Oxford. Mr Coulombe is a member of the Keys (the Catholic Writers' Guild) and the Mythopoeic Society, an organization dedicated to the study of the works of J. R. R. Tolkien and C. S. Lewis. He has two books to his credit, and his work on religion, politics and folklore has appeared in journals in his native land, Great Britain, Ireland, France, Germany, Canada, Australia, New Zealand, and South Africa.

The late Mr Paul Edwin Zimmer, of Greyhaven, remarked to me once that most analysis of the work of J. R. R. Tolkien was undertaken from the Evangelical Protestant or from the Anglican point of view. As Tolkien himself was a fervent Catholic, he reasoned, a Catholic critique might shed new light. Thus encouraged, I began.

It will be the contention of the paper that much of Mr Tolkien's unique vision was directly shaped by recurring images in the Catholic culture which shaped JRRT, and which are not shared by non-Catholics generally. The expression of these images in *The Lord of the Rings* will then concern us.

To begin with, it must be remembered that Catholic culture and Catholic faith, while mutually supportive and symbiotic, are not the same thing. Mr Walker Percy, in his *Lost in the Cosmos*, explored the difference, and pointed out that, culturally, Catholics in Cleveland are much more Protestant than Presbyterians in say, Taos, New Orleans, or the South of France. Erik ritter von Kuehnelt-Leddihn, points out the effects of this dichotomy upon politics, attributing the multi-party system in Catholic countries to the Catholic adherence to absolutes; he further ascribes the two-party system to the Protestant willingness to compromise. However this may be, it does point up a constant element in Catholic thought – the pursuit of the absolute.

Here we must make an aside in regard to the US. Catholic culture in America is practically non-existent, except in attenuated form among such peoples as the Hispanos and Indians of Northern New Mexico, the Cajuns and Creoles of Louisiana and other Gulf States, and the old English Catholic settlements of Maryland and Kentucky. Elsewhere, the Faith was brought by immigrants, and its attendant culture has, like all imported ones in the States, veered between preservation and assimilation. This was exacerbated by the fact that Catholic leadership in the United States was early committed to a programme of cultural melding. In addition, this leadership was primarily Irish, a nationality which had been deprived of much of its native culture by centuries of Protestant ascendancy. Hence it has been extremely difficult for Americans, even American Catholics, to understand or appreciate the Catholic *thing* (as Chesterton described it) in a cultural context. I am reminded of the astonishment of a classmate of mine (from a typical American Catholic high school) at seeing an anthology of Catholic poetry. This situation has been greatly accentuated in the past twenty years by the changes occurring after Vatican II.

This being so, it will be necessary to describe a little of the uniquely Catholic world-view. In fine, it is a sacramental one. At the heart of all Catholic life is a miracle, a mystery, the Blessed Sacrament. Surrounded traditionally by ritual and awe, it has been the formative aspect of Catholic art, drama, and poetry. The coronation of kings, swearing of oaths, marriages, celebrations of feast-days, all have a Eucharistic character. Before the advent of Cartesianism, it was held (among other and higher things) to be the highest act of Magic, before which all other acts of theurgy, goetia or sympathetic magic were as nought. It was the unitive force of the Catholic world, mystically uniting in sacrificial bond all the altars across the globe.

This great miracle was held to be prefigured by the sacrifice of the Jewish temple, and indeed to have been foreseen in some dim way by the mysteries and philosophies of the ancient world. Hence nothing that was not evil in these older faiths was rejected out of hand, although a clear distinction was made between them and Catholicism.

Under this influence, Catholic societies were societies of wonder. Life was held to be a series of miracles. With God Himself appearing on the altar, in consumable form, how difficult were wizards, elves or the change of seasons? As Aragorn replied to Éothain: 'The green earth, say you? That is a mighty matter of legend, though you tread it under the light of day!' So might reply any European of the past, or a Cajun, Galwayman, Sicilian, Micmac, Tagalog, Alfur, or Baganda of today. It is this quality which leads us to dub those peoples 'mythopoeic', and their modern equivalents 'superstitious' or 'backward'.

Politically, traditional Catholic culture has been hierarchical. Feudalism itself was formed in the great degree by the Faith, as is shown by the great difference between the feudal system of European history, and its equivalents in the India of the Mughals, the Japan of the Tokugawa, and the China of the Warring States. Ideas of chivalry and hierarchy suggested by the Church did not merely shape European Catholic polity, but continue to determine political structures in such settings as Catholicized African tribes, ethnic Catholic Asian settlements, and Latin America. The relationships of king to subject, of lord to vassal, of comrade to comrade-in-arms remain, though often under other names.

In traditional Catholic societies, the king is, in a lessened sense, the Vicar of God. While not approximating the sacral kingship of non-Catholic peoples, the Catholic monarchy nevertheless retains a certain sacredness. This remains the case, even when in conflict with the Church. After the calamities of the Reformation, English Civil War, Glorious, French, Industrial, and Russian Revolutions, etc., the king became more than that; he became the exiled leader of the faithful, whose return alone would bring a return to the old ways, and an end to change and unrest.

These various themes continue to affect Catholic consciousness today. We will observe how far Tolkien was a cultural as well as a doctrinal Catholic (despite being raised in a Protestant land) and how these themes emerge in *The Lord of the Rings*.

The Birmingham Oratory which provided the backdrop of JRRT's life from 1904 to 1911, was founded by Cardinal Newman and remained a stronghold of cultural Catholicism. Fr Francis Morgan, JRRT's guardian, he described as a 'Welsh–Spanish Tory', surely as ultramontane a combination as one could wish for. Even today, with some few exceptions, the houses of the Oratory around the world are renowned for both orthodoxy and learning. It was here that our author's religious sense was formed, and during this time that his literary and linguistic interests began. Later, his studies were confined primarily to works of the pre-Reformation. Beyond Chaucer, he had little interest. Judging by his later work, his early environment and studies supplied that which would have been supplied had he lived in a Catholic country. Had he lived away from the Oratory, a living example of Catholic culture, one wonders what the effect on his work would have been.

In the sphere of doctrine, of course, the influence of Catholicism upon JRRT is readily apparent. In this regard he himself admitted as much, when he wrote in a letter to Deborah Webster of 25 October 1958, 'far greater things may colour the mind in dealing with the lesser things of a fairy-story'.

The Blessed Sacrament was very much at the heart of JRRT's devotional life. As he informs his son on p. 339 of his *Collected Letters*:

> I myself am convinced by the Petrine claims, nor looking around the world does there seem much doubt which (if Christianity is true) is the True Church, the temple of the Spirit dying but living, corrupt but holy, self-reforming and rearising. But for me that Church of which the Pope is the acknowledged head on earth has as chief claim that it is the one that has (and still does) ever defended the Blessed Sacrament, and given it most honour, and put (as Christ plainly intended) in the prime place. 'Feed my sheep' was His last charge to St. Peter; and since His words are always first to be understood literally, I suppose them to refer primarily to the Bread of Life. It was against this that the W. European revolt (or Reformation) was really launched – 'the blasphemous fable of the Mass' – and faith/works a mere red herring.

This one finds echoed in the figure of *lembas*, which 'had a potency that increased as travellers relied on it alone, and did not mingle it with other goods. It fed the will, and it gave strength to endure' (Vol. 3, p. 262). This is all very reminiscent of the large literature of Eucharistic miracles, and of such people as St Lydwine, St Francis Borgia, and Theresa Neumann, who lived off only the Blessed Sacrament.

Another unique feature of Catholic life which distinguishes it from that of other Christians is the veneration of the Blessed Virgin Mary, which JRRT shared enthusiastically.

As an example, we cite a letter to Robert Murray, SJ, in which he speaks of 'Our Lady, upon which all my own small perception of beauty, both in majesty and simplicity is founded'. To a degree in the figure of Galadriel, but more particularly in that of Elbereth may one discern the shadow of Mary:

> Snow-white! Snow-white! O Lady clear!
> O Queen beyond the Western Seas!
> O Light to us that wander here
> Amid the world of woven trees!
>
> Gilthoniel! O Elbereth!
> Clear are thy eyes and bright thy breath,
> Snow-white! Snow-white! We sing to thee
> In a far land beyond the sea.
>
> O stars that in the Sunless Year
> With shining hand by her were sown,
> In windy fields now bright and clear
> We see your silver blossom blown!
>
> O Elbereth! Gilthoniel!
> We still remember, we who dwell
> In this far land beneath the trees,
> Thy starlight on the Western Seas.

One is immediately reminded of the English hymn by John Lingard, with which JRRT was certainly familiar:

> Hail, Queen of Heaven, the ocean star,
> Guide of the wand'rer here below:
> Thrown on life's surge, we claim thy care –
> save us from peril and from woe.
> Mother of Christ, star of the sea,
> Pray for the wanderer, pray for me.

Sojourners in this vale of tears,
To thee, blest advocate, we cry;
Pity our sorrows, calm our fears,
And soothe with hope our misery.
Refuge in grief, star of the sea,
Pray for the mourner, pray for me.

As earlier observed, the Catholic view of the world is a sacramental one; the centre of Catholic life, according to C. G. Jung, 'is a living mystery, and that is the thing that works'. Opponents of the Church have often claimed that the sacraments are 'mere' magic. The phrase *hocus pocus* is a parody of the words of consecration, *Hoc est enim corpus meum*. As Galadriel observes, 'this is what your folk would call magic, I believe; though I do not understand clearly what they mean; and they seem also to use the same words of the deceits of the enemy'. Indeed, one may go so far as to say that the effect of magic, wielded for good, is in *The Lord of the Rings* the same as that of the Sacraments upon the life of the devout Catholic. Protection, nourishment, knowledge, all are held to flow in supernatural abundance from them. In his prayer after communion, St Thomas Aquinas asks that the Blessed Sacrament be 'a strong defence against the snares of all enemies, visible and invisible'. St Bonaventure declares it to be 'the fountain of life, the fountain of wisdom and knowledge, the fountain of eternal light'. In a word, as the Sacraments are the means of Grace in the Catholic world, magic – wielded by the wise – is the means of Grace in Middle-earth.

The sacraments are the centre and cause of all authentic Catholic mysticism, and the saints have owed their remarkable careers to them. Certainly, in terms of the physical phenomena of mysticism (Eucharistic miracles; ecstasies; the stigmata; levitation; bilocation; luminous irradiance; supernatural fragrances; infused knowledge; vision through opaque bodies; supernatural power over objects, etc.) the great mystics have often performed wonders worthy of Gandalf and Elrond (one thinks of St Jean Vianney, the Curé d'Ars, for example, or of Padre Pio). This too is something of which JRRT would have been aware. As Arthur Machen observed, the only realities are sanctity and sorcery.

From the realm of myth, magic, and mystery, we now descend to that of history. There is a particularly Catholic view of history, summed up by JRRT in a letter to Amy Ronald of 15 December 1956: 'actually, I'm a Christian, and indeed a Roman Catholic, so that I do not expect "history" to be anything but a long defeat – though it contains (and in a legend may contain more clearly and movingly) some samples or glimpses of final victory'.

In the range of modern Catholic history, there are certain archetypes, which, it may be argued, are reflected in *The Lord of the Rings*, in the manner he described. The ones we will examine are: (a) the age of faith, or the organic state; (b) Church versus State; (c) the great king; (d) the onset of modernity and the martyr-king; (e) the restoration (successful or otherwise).

The concept of society as an organic whole, without class conflict, with a communal structure, is one that has characterized Catholic social thought since the Roman Empire. In many ways the Shire expresses perfectly the economic and political ideals of the Church, as expressed by Leo XIII in *Rerum novarum*, and Pius XI in *Quadragesimo anno*. Traditional authority (the Thain), limited except in times of crisis; popular representation (the Mayor of Michel Delving), likewise limited; subsidiarity; and above all, minimal organization and conflict. It is the sort of society envisioned by Distributists Belloc and Chesterton in Britain, by Salazar in Portugal, by the framers of the Irish Constitution, by Dollfuss in Austria, and by Smetone in Lithuania. However far short or close these dwellers in the real world came to their goal, the fact remains that it is something very close to the Shire they had in mind.

In the ages of faith, while both Church and State were dedicated to roughly the same ends, they often differed as to how to go about achieving them. Then too, human nature and greed often sowed discord. Sometimes the life-and-death struggle with Islam was hindered by these quarrels. In *The Lord of the Rings*, we see these struggles reflected in the tension between Gandalf and Denethor II. Gandalf, indeed, partakes of much of the nature of the Papacy. He belongs to no one nation, and in a very real sense he is leader of all the free and faithful. This is so because his power is magical rather than temporal, just as the Pope's is sacramental. Denethor's interest is wholly national. To his statement 'there is no purpose higher in the world as it now stands than the good of Gondor', Gandalf replies, 'the rule of no realm is mine, neither Gondor nor any other, great or small. But all worthy things that are in peril as the world now stands, those are my care ... For I also am a steward.' Thus might Boniface VIII have spoken to Philip the Fair, or Gregory VII to Henry IV, or Innocent III to King John. Gandalf also reminds one of the Fisher-King in the Grail legends, who himself is a symbol of Peter-in-the-Boat.

On the other hand, the Catholic imagination was also haunted by the image of the great kings, like Arthur, St Ferdinand III, and St Louis IX. These were held to have been the ideal prototypes for rulers: pious, brave, wonderful in a manner unapproachable for those of later times. In three characters in particular, Elendil, Gil-Galad, and Durin, do we find the yearning for the great king in terms with which western Catholics of yesteryear and Third World Catholics of today would be familiar:

> Gil-Galad was an Elven-King.
> Of him the harpers sadly sing!
> The last whose realm was fair and free
> Between the Mountains and the Sea.

and again:

> The world was young, the mountains green,
> No stain yet on the moon was seen.
> No words were laid on stream or stone,
> When Durin woke and walked alone.
>
> The world was fair, the mountains tall,
> In Elder days before the fall
> Of mighty kings in Nargothrond
> and Gondolin who now beyond
> Western Seas have passed away:
> The world was fair in Durin's day.

So might a medieval minstrel have mourned the Nine Worthies; so might a modern one mourn the Negus, or the Mwami, or the Kabaka. The forms change, but for a Catholic, the subject rarely does.

The upheavals earlier referred to destroyed Catholic unity, splintered society, and destroyed much that was beautiful. The enclosures and various other economic measures ended western society's communal nature. The great present-day expressions of these forces of modernity are capitalism and communism, with all they represent. JRRT's feelings about such things are clear. In *The Hobbit*, we are told of Goblins that 'they invented some of the machines that have since troubled our world, especially the ingenious devices for killing large numbers of people at once, for wheels and engines and explosions have always delighted them'. Of course, the descriptions given in 'The Scouring of the Shire' are particularly apropos.

In the struggle between tradition and modernity, three famous monarchs lost their lives: Charles I, Louis XVI, and Nicholas II. While the first and last were not officially Catholics, they were at least culturally so. Traditional forces in England, France, and Russia were solemnly canonized by the Anglican and Russian Orthodox Churches; Louis XVI is still regarded as a martyr by thousands of French royalists. Each owed their deaths to two items: a desire to uphold the traditional constitution of Church and State in their respective realms, and a personal weakness or flaw which reduced their effectiveness in so doing. They also shared heroic deaths which, to a great degree, redeemed their mistakes in the eyes of many of their subjects. All of this applies to Isildur as well.

The social ideas earlier referred to were contradicted by the events of history. With their end as fact, they became hope. This hope became concentrated in the cause of the deposed sovereign, who would, upon his return to power, set all things to rights again:

> 'Till then, upon Ararat's hill
> My hope shall cast her anchor still
> Until I see some peaceful dove,
> Bring home the branch she dearly love;
> Then will I wait, till the waters abate,
> Which now disturb my troubled brain:
> Else never rejoice, till I hear the voice,
> That the King enjoys his own again.

As time passed, the claims went to heirs, but the ever hopeful adherents continued their struggle. Thus, the Jacobites fought for the Stuarts in 1689–90, 1715, 1719, and 1745–46; the Carlists in Spain rebelled in 1833–39, during the 1840s and 50s, and in 1872–76. They also played a key role in the Spanish Civil War on the Nationalist side. The Chouans and the Vendeens continued guerrilla warfare against the French Republic all through the Revolution; even today, French royalism flourishes. The Miguelists of Portugal continued their agitation against first the liberal monarchy and then the republic down to the present. Since the fall of the Austro-Hungarian Empire, Habsburg adherents have pursued dreams of restoration. So greatly did Hitler fear this possibility that he named the planned invasion of Austria *Case Otto*, after the exiled heir. Whatever may become of their political hopes, the canonization of Charles, the last Emperor, may be presaged by the incorruptibility of his remains at Madeira.

However this may be, such people looked to a restoration to restore the Church to prominence, curb industry, revive the smallholder and the old order of society. As Robert Burns observed:

> The Church is in ruins, the State is in jars,
> delusions, oppressions, and murderous wars.
> We dare nae well say it, but we ken wha's to blame,
> There'll never be peace 'till Jamie comes hame.

As it became apparent that Jamie would not come home, nor would Don Carlos, nor Dom Miguel, nor the Comte de Chambord, many looked for less regal saviours. From such desires emerged (and emerge) such men as Franco, Pilsudski, and many of the better Latin American Caudillos. In a sense, this Catholic political messianism is even present in the careers of such diverse figures as Kennedy and Castro.

Aragorn succeeds where Bonnie Prince Charlie and the others failed. Instead of the field of Culloden's defeat and mourning, we have the field of Cormallen's victory and rejoicing. In Middle-earth, the 'good old cause' triumphs. The Dúnedain, so like the Jacobites, Carlists, and Legitimists for most of their history, gain at last the victory. From being the Young Pretender, Aragorn becomes Charlemagne, restorer of the Empire. Indeed, his restored kingdom has much in common with the Carolingian Renaissance. It would not be unfair to say that it is this which Catholics have at the bottom of their minds when they consider things political. In

Middle-earth, all things do become well, for the King enjoys his own again.

There are other symbols: the dark Lord's forces might represent not only modernity, but the Islam which was Christendom's greatest previous enemy; the Tower of Guard, Minas Tirith, might be seen as a symbol of the Church Militant, of the *Res Publica Christiana*. But we have examined a few of the most evocative motifs in terms of the Catholic psyche.

In his *Hieroglyphics: Notes on the Ecstatic in Literature*, Mr Arthur Machen declares, 'Literature is the expression, through the artistic medium of words, of the dogmas of the Catholic Church, and that which is in any way out of harmony with these dogmas is not literature,' for 'Catholic dogma is merely the witness, under a special symbolism of the enduring facts of human nature and the universe.' Whether or no JRRT would have agreed with this definition, he did say, in the letter to Fr Murray, SJ, already cited, '*Lord of the Rings* is of course a fundamentally religious and Catholic work; unconsciously so at first, but consciously in the revision ... For the religious element is absorbed into the story and the symbolism.'

It has been said that the dominant note of the traditional Catholic liturgy was intense longing. This is also true of her art, her literature, her whole life. It is a longing for things that cannot be in this world: unearthly truth, unearthly purity, unearthly justice, unearthly beauty. By all these earmarks *The Lord of the Rings* is indeed a Catholic work, as its author believed; but it is more. It is this age's great Catholic epic, fit to stand beside the Grail legends, *Le Morte D'Arthur*, and *The Canterbury Tales*. It is at once a great comfort to the individual Catholic, and a tribute to the enduring power and greatness of the Catholic tradition, that JRRT created this work. In an age which has seen almost total rejection of the Faith on the part of the civilization she created, the loss of the Faith on the part of many lay Catholics, and apparent uncertainty among her hierarchy, *The Lord of the Rings* assures us, both by its existence and its message, that the darkness cannot triumph forever.

6

ON THE REALITY OF FANTASY
JAMES V. SCHALL SJ

James V. Schall SJ is Professor of Government at Georgetown University, Washington, DC. His article first appeared in the March 1992 issue of Crisis.

By chance, just before leaving my brother's in Santa Cruz in January, I happened to notice an article in the San Jose *Mercury-News* commemorating the one-hundredth anniversary of the birth of J. R. R. Tolkien. The article noted that a number of elaborate editions of Tolkien's works are being published this year. It also identified several societies devoted to the study of Tolkien, among which are the 'Mythopoeic Society', the 'Elvish Linguistic Fellowship', and the 'American Tolkien Society'.

The founder of the Mythopoeic Society, Glen Good-Knight, is cited as remarking that 'Tolkien is considered the grandfather of the modern fantasy phenomena. Go into the science-fiction section [of a book store] and half are fantasy.' Tolkien, no doubt, is full of elves, hobbits, dwarves, and all sorts of awesome races of beings. Yet, I could not help but think that to assign Tolkien to the category of mere 'fantasy' somehow missed the essence of what he was about. I have always found in reading Tolkien a certain doom or dread strangely combined with a certain joy and exhilaration precisely because he was talking about something very real, about the way this, yes, fantastic world really is.

Several years ago now, I was in a used book store in San Francisco down near the end of Ellis Street, I think. For reasons I forget, I had wanted to obtain a copy of Tolkien's *The Silmarillion*. After I had looked all over this vast chaotic place by myself, a friend who was with me called down from a ladder over against the west wall to come over. I was triumphantly handed a hardback edition of *The Silmarillion*. I was frankly astonished.

This particular edition, amusingly, was published by the Bookcase Shop in Taipei in 1977. It cost $2 used and was (and still is) in good condition. 'This is an authorized Taiwan Edition reprinted by permission of the publisher (George Allen and Unwin) for sale in Taiwan only. It is not to be exported.' Well, we were definitely not on Taiwan. But, as I told my friend who found the book later, 'I have never read anything quite so beautiful as the first page of *The Silmarillion*, the chapter entitled "Ainulindalë: The Music of the Ainur".' I like to read it or have it read aloud.

In the book, the previous owner, perhaps the one who pirated it out of Taipei, had inserted a review of *The Silmarillion* from the 11 September 1977 Chicago *Tribune*. The review was by Roger Sale, a professor at the University of Washington who wrote a book called *Tolkien and Frodo Baggins*. Sale did not think many people would like this book in comparison to *The Lord of the Rings*, which sold as many as fifty million copies. He added, 'Tolkien was one of those moderns who, in his twentieth-century darkness, was driven to invent an earlier time when the world was fresh, the sky clear, the grass green and the past was important'. Again, I thought, this observation surely misses the point Tolkien was driving at. Tolkien was not escaping from the twentieth century. Just as his 'fantasy' was not apart from reality. Tolkien, I suspect, thought that what was going on in the twentieth century was just what was going on in his stories.

The end of *The Hobbit* reads like this:

'Then the prophecies of the old songs have turned out to be true, after a fashion!' said Bilbo.

'Of course!' said Gandalf. 'And why should not they prove true? Surely you don't disbelieve the prophecies, because you had a hand in bringing them about yourself? You don't really suppose, do you, that all your adventures and escapes were managed by mere luck, just for your sole benefit? You are a very fine person, Mr Baggins, and I am very fond of you; but you are only quite a little fellow in a wide world after all!'

'Thank goodness' said Bilbo laughing, and handed him the tobacco-jar.

If we look at the 'teaching', at the truth of what is being said in this passage, we might be somewhat cautious to intimate that this book is merely 'fantasy', merely an escape from the twentieth century. Nor is it a fiction dreamed up by a rather dotty Oxford don that would later give hope for the sixties, as the article in the San Jose paper seemed to imply. What Tolkien was about and what the sixties were about seem almost to be total opposites, however much the illusions of the sixties would not have surprised a Tolkien.

The teaching of Gandalf is that we are part of an order, a providence. Simply because we are involved in adventure and escape does not mean that we are the sole actors in our lives. The world is very wide, and what benefits us does not merely benefit us alone, just as what hurts us does not merely hurt us. Bilbo's response to this teaching – 'Thank goodness' – is a very contented, Christian one. It implies that the whole burden of the world is not on us, even if we are ourselves involved in the agonies and drama of the world with its struggles of good and evil.

In his famous essay 'On Fairy Stories', Tolkien himself explained some of the deeper meaning that should cause us to hesitate to think that somehow such fantasy is not dealing with reality, our reality. 'It is often reported of fairies (truly or lyingly, I do not know) that they are workers of illusions, that they are cheaters of men by "fantasy"; but that is quite another matter,' Tolkien wrote. 'Such trickeries happen, at any rate, inside tales in which the fairies are not themselves illusions; behind the fantasy real wills and powers exist, independent of the minds and purposes of men.'

This is heady stuff, no doubt – real wills and powers exist independent of the minds and purposes of men, yet, as Gandalf said to Bilbo, not excluding them either. Tolkien remarks in the same essay that we must accept the inside of the fairy story as true in its plot and order. If we break the spell of its story, we lose what it is saying.

When we come, however, to the conclusion of this remarkable essay – which was originally a lecture given at St Andrew's in Scotland in 1937 and later enlarged and included in *Essays in Honour of Charles Williams* – we see that Tolkien is about something of far more serious purpose than we might think if we allow ourselves to think of 'fantasy' in a superficial manner. If there are stories and tales in the world of Tolkien's characters, there are tales and stories in our world, too. If Tolkien 'creates' a world, he reminds us that the accounts of Creation and Redemption as they appear in our tradition contain a striking truth about them. 'The Gospels contain a fairy-story, or a story of a larger kind which embraces all the essence of fairy-stories.' Moreover, it is a story that has 'entered history'.

The difficulty of this story that we find in Scripture, when seen from the point of view of its plausibility as fantasy, is that it is too true, too much like what we would want if we could have it.

There is no tale ever told that men would rather find was true, and none which so many sceptical men have accepted as true on its own merits. For the Art of it has the supremely convincing tone of Primary Art, that is, of Creation. To reject it leads either to sadness or to wrath.

This latter remark about rejection explains why central to all Tolkien's characters of whatever nature is the will, the power to choose, to accept or to reject. Without this, there is no drama, no fairy-story, no human or angelic life. If the world is full of sadness and wrath, as it no doubt is, it is because it is full of will. This is why fairy-stories, like life itself, include both doom and glory.

Tolkien ends the essay 'On Fairy Stories' with these lines whose power is almost overwhelming:

> But in God's kingdom the presence of the greatest does not depress the small. Redeemed Man is still man. Story, fantasy, still go on, and should go on. The Evangelium has not abrogated the legends; it has hallowed them, especially the 'happy ending'. The Christian has still to work, with mind as well as body, to suffer, hope, and die; but he may now perceive that all his bents and faculties have a purpose which can be redeemed.

Tolkien's world contains diversity even of virtue. He sees that the real temptation against which fairy-stories are written is the despair that in the end there is no happy ending. But it is also written with the clear, if paradoxical, knowledge that if in the end there is indeed no happiness, it is because of our wills. Fairy-tales, as Tolkien said, 'enrich' creation. The unsuspecting reader who thinks he is only reading 'fantasy' in reading Tolkien will suddenly find himself pondering the state of his own soul because he recognizes his own soul in each fairy-tale.

In the 'real' world, then, like the 'fantasy' world, is there some 'imagination' in which the tales of Genesis and John may be 'true'? The 'fallen', real world we know, is this all there is? And do we, like Bilbo Baggins, remain in it, in the stories? 'All tales may come true; and yet, at the last, redeemed, they may be as like and as unlike the forms that we give them as Man, finally redeemed, will be like and unlike the fallen that we know.' There is something uncanny here, when the greatest fantasy writer of our time hints that the truth of fantasy is justified because 'the prophecies of the old songs have turned out to be true'. On the first page of *The Silmarillion*, we read:

> Then Ilúvatar said to them [the Ainur, His first created beings]: 'Of the theme that I have declared to you, I will now that ye make in harmony together a Great Music. And since I have kindled you with the Flame Imperishable, ye shall show forth your powers in adorning this theme, each with his own thoughts and devices, if he will. But I will sit and hearken, and be glad that through you great beauty has been wakened into song.'

All the great Tolkien themes are already here – the dignity of creation, of finite beings, awe, will, hence potential doom or glory, providence, beauty, desire, order, grace, joy.

There is no tale ever told that men would rather find to be true. To reject it leads either to sadness or to wrath. Surely you don't disbelieve the prophecies because you had a hand in bringing them about yourself?

7

J. R. R. TOLKIEN: A MYTHOLOGY FOR ENGLAND
ELWIN FAIRBURN

Elwin Fairburn might be considered something of a hobbit himself. Apart from Tolkien, whom he discovered in his late teens, his interests include real ale, morris dancing, and history, both local and natural. Although he now earns his living in the decidedly unhobbitish profession of computer programming, he notes without surprise that as he grows older the hair on his toes is growing steadily longer and curlier!

On 3 January 1892, in the dusty frontier town of Bloemfontein, in the Afrikaaner Republic of the Oranje Vrystaat, an expatriate English bank manager's wife gave birth to her first child. A hundred years later that child, John Ronald Reuel Tolkien, would be honoured across the world. He would be honoured especially for his epic heroic romance, *The Lord of the Rings*, which since its publication in the mid-1950s has given joy and inspiration to millions on a scale denied to his predecessors this century in the heroic romance genre – Lord Dunsany, E. R. Eddison, James Branch Cabell and David Lindsay – or to the host of successors and sometimes imitators he has inspired. They too offered 'escapism', a refuge in pleasant fantasy from an ever less pleasant twentieth-century reality. As Tolkien himself said, there is nothing wrong with escapism if one is in jail, and he would have been the first to denounce our times as among the worst spiritual jails in human history. But none of the other fantasy writers, offering escapism alone, has come close to rivalling

Tolkien's enduring appeal. Clearly, he had struck a nerve deeper in the psyche of our modern 'Western' civilization. But what was it? What is the secret of Tolkien's success?

Firstly, he offered his readers a clear sense of cultural and ethnic identity, reflecting his own clear sense of his own such identity. He described this to his American publishers thus: 'I am indeed in English terms a West-Midlander at home only in the counties upon the Welsh Marches; and it is, I believe, as much due to descent as to opportunity that Anglo-Saxon and Western Middle English and alliterative verse have been both a childhood attraction and my main professional sphere.' He admitted an eighteenth-century German ancestor (hence his un-English surname) but added that his family were 'intensely English (not British)'.[1]

To W. H. Auden he stressed that he was 'a West-Midlander by blood (and took to early west-midland Middle English as a known tongue as soon as I set eyes on it)'.[2] He stressed to his son Christopher that 'barring the Tolkien (which must long ago have become a pretty thin strand) you are a Mercian of Hwiccian (of Wychwood) on both sides'.[3] To another of his sons, Michael, he wrote that 'any corner of that county' – Worcestershire, whence his mother's ancestry sprang – 'is in an indefinable way "home" to me, as no other part of the world is'.[4] This sense of identity inspired a deep love of his homeland: 'I love England,' he told his son, '(not Great Britain and certainly not the British Commonwealth (grr!)).'[5]

This intense awareness of his Englishness, specifically his Mercianness, suffused Tolkien's novels, especially *The Lord of the Rings*, but also *The Hobbit* and, more subtly as we shall see, *The Silmarillion*. For as its creator repeatedly stressed, particularly in some notes he wrote on a review of the third volume of *The Lord of the Rings* by W. H. Auden in 1956, his 'Middle-Earth is not an imaginary world'. Not only is it very much a part of our own world, 'the North-West of the Old World, east of the Sea'.[7] But, as far as the Shire, the idealized rustic homeland of Tolkien's hobbit heroes is concerned, Tolkien's own part of our world: 'The Shire is based on rural England and no other country in the world.'[8] Indeed, Tolkien's particular area of rural England: the Shire 'is in fact more or less a Warwickshire village of about the period of the Diamond Jubilee'.[9]

So closely anchored was Tolkien's sub-creation in his own sense of local identity that he observed of his childhood in Sarehole, a (then!) rural Warwickshire village south of Birmingham that he 'lived for my early years in "the Shire" in a pre-mechanical age'.[10] The names of places in the Shire, Tolkien observed somewhat later, 'are in fact devised according to the style, origins and mode of formation of English (especially Midland) place names'.[11] Even Bilbo's and Frodo's home is in Mercia: 'Bag End was the local name for my aunt's farm in Worcestershire, which was at the end of a lane leading to it and no further.'[12]

As the land at the heart of *The Lord of the Rings* was his land, so the folk who are its heroes are his own folk – sprung from England – specifically Mercian England, the Midlands. He once told an interviewer: 'The hobbits are just rustic English people, made small in size because it reflects the generally small reach of their imagination – not the small reach of their courage or latent power.'[13] Tolkien had witnessed this courage and latent power when, as a Second Lieutenant in the Lancashire Fusiliers, he had fought in the carnage of the Battle of the Somme in 1916, where most of his school friends died. He tried to do it justice in his depiction of the rustic hobbit Sam Gamgee, Frodo's loyal companion, who is one of the best-loved characters in *The Lord of the Rings*. 'My "Sam Gamgee",' Tolkien later revealed, 'is indeed a reflection of the English soldier, of the privates and batmen I knew in the 1914 war, and recognised as so far superior to myself.'[14] On another occasion he expressed his delight in 'the Englishry of this jewel among the hobbits'.[15]

It is not only the hobbits who are drawn from the deep well of Tolkien's own Englishness. The enigmatic Tom Bombadil was envisaged by his creator as 'the spirit of the (vanishing) Oxford and Berkshire countryside'.[16] The Riders of Rohan do not merely speak Old English – 'Anglo-Saxon' – but, as Professor T. A. Shippey, a successor of Tolkien as Professor of English Language and Medieval Literature at Leeds University, has observed, they speak specifically Mercian Old English: 'Saruman, Hasufel, Herugrim for "standard" Searuman, Heasufel, Heorugrim'.[17] The fact that the Riders spoke the same tongue as Tolkien's Mercian ancestors was further exemplified by their own name for their own land, 'The Mark', which was also the name by which Tolkien's forebears had known their West Midlands homeland. This was later dog-Latinized to 'Mercia' by Wessex-accented monks who called it 'Mearc' rather than 'Mark'. The other heroes of Tolkien's epic are likewise visibly sprung from English soil and spirit, or, in the case of Gandalf, whom Tolkien thought of as 'the Odinic wanderer',[18] that of the kindred North which Tolkien also loved.

Tolkien once wrote that 'if you want to write a tale of this sort you must consult your roots',[19] and it is this deep sense of his own cultural and ethnic identity which distinguishes his writing from much other modern 'heroic fantasy'. The sheer cultural richness and diversity of Tolkien's Middle-earth, with its peoples, languages, lore and thousands of years of recorded history, is magnificent. But that is not all there is to Tolkien. He offers not just the magnificence of imagination rooted in an ancient and real culture, his own, but also a purpose: a myth and a manifesto. Tolkien's sense of what he was became the source not only of what he wrote but why he wrote it; and ultimately why what he wrote is not just a fine story but a relevant message. Tolkien was trying to do more than tell a story. He was trying to lay the foundations of a myth. A national myth. 'A mythology for England.'[20]

His dream began in his youth. In 1912, whilst a twenty-year-old undergraduate at Exeter College, Oxford, Tolkien read a paper to a college society on the *Kalevala*, the great Finnish national mythopoeic epic. This epic, or national myth, had been recreated from ancient folktales by Elias Lonnrot in the early nineteenth century and, even as Tolkien spoke, was playing a powerful role in transforming the Finns from apathetic Russian, and earlier Swedish, provincials into a reawakened nation. He concluded by lamenting, 'I would we had more of it left – something of the same sort that belonged to the English.'[21] From this arose his great project, as he put it, 'to make a body of more or less connected legend, ranging from the large and cosmogonic, to the level of romantic fairy-story – the larger founded on the lesser in contact with the earth, the lesser drawing splendour from the vast backcloths – which I could dedicate simply: to England; to my country'.[22]

To his country, to England, Tolkien dedicated first the epic mythos later published as *The Silmarillion* and then the tales it in turn inspired, *The Lord of the Rings* and *The Hobbit*. As Professor Shippey has observed, 'Tolkien's grand design, or desire, was to give back to his own country the legends that had been taken from it in the Dark Ages after the Conquest'[23] – a Norman Conquest which, his biographer remarked, 'pained him as much as if it had happened in his lifetime'.[24] His plan was 'to draw some of the great tales in fullness, and leave many only placed in the scheme, and sketched. The cycles should be linked to a majestic whole, and yet leave scope for other minds and hands, wielding paint and music and drama.'[25] He later called his grand plan 'absurd' but no review would, perhaps, have pleased him more than that which the *Guardian* gave *The Silmarillion* when it appeared four years after the author's death: 'How, given little over half a century of work, did one man become the creative equivalent of a people?' Or the *Financial Times*: 'at times rises to the greatness of true myth'.

Whether such praise was merited, whether Tolkien did in fact lay the foundations of a 'mythology for England' is moot, and for the future to decide. It may well be that nations alone give birth to national mythologies, not isolated individuals born, as Tolkien himself lamented, 'in a dark age, out of due time'.[26] Either way, Tolkien certainly believed that England had entered a 'dark age' as dire in its implications as that which he believed had followed the Norman Conquest. This was expressed in 1943 in a letter to his son Christopher, then serving in the RAF:

> the bigger things get the smaller and duller or flatter the globe gets. It is getting to be all one blasted little provincial suburb. When they have introduced American sanitation, morale-pep, feminism and mass-production throughout the Near East, Far East, USSR, the Pampas, el Gran Chaco, the Danubian Basin, Equatorial Africa, Hither, Further and Inner Mumbo-land, Gondhwanaland, Lhasa and the villages of darkest Berkshire, how happy we shall be. At any rate it ought to cut down travel. There will be nowhere to go ... Col. Knox says one-eighth of the world's population speaks 'English' and that it is the biggest language group. If true, damn shame – say I. May the curse of Babel strike all their tongues till they can only say 'baa-baa'. It would mean much the same. I think I shall have to refuse to speak anything but Old Mercian. But seriously: I do find this Americo-cosmopolitanism very terrifying ...[27]

'Americo-cosmopolitanism' was not the only aspect of the world around him which revolted Tolkien. As the critic Roger Sale observed, 'Tolkien has always spoken ... as though only fools and madmen would contemplate the twentieth century without horror.'[28] The result is that, as another critic, Colin Wilson, put it:

> *The Lord of the Rings* is a criticism of the modern world
> and of the values of technological civilization. It asserts its
> own values, and tries to persuade the reader that they are
> preferable to current values. Even the 'poetry', which
> everybody admits to be no better than average, underlines
> the feeling of seriousness, that even if the landscapes and
> adventures bear a superficial resemblance to Edgar Rice
> Burroughs' Martian novels, the purpose goes deeper. This,
> I think, defines what my early informants about the book
> were unable to explain: why it can be taken so seriously. In
> fact, like *The Waste Land*, it is at once an attack on the
> modern world and a credo, a manifesto.[29]

It is a manifesto for a world as far removed from the values of
'Americo-cosmopolitanism' as it is possible to imagine. A
world of identities and hierarchies and nobility and beauty
and heroism. A world in which every one of the Free Peoples
– Elves, Dwarves, Hobbits, Ents, and the various nations of
Men – has its own culture and homeland and history and
hence sense of worth. They each preserve, without mutual
hostility, their own speech and way of life and ethnicity. As
Professor Paul Kocher of Stanford University explains,
'Tolkien does not desiderate any such mingling of species as
will erode the special identity of each ... the coexistence of
the free peoples of Middle-earth is founded on mutual respect
and co-operation.'[30] It is a world which is based, as Professor
Shippey observes, like that of *Beowulf* and the Norse sagas,
on 'the conviction that people are their heredity'.[31]

It follows that, as Professor Walter Scheps has commented,
'the only egalitarian wind which blows through the sentient
trees of Middle-earth comes from the East, and the egalitari-
anism of which it brings tidings is in foul slavery'.[32] The
nearest thing to a 'western-style democracy' in *The Lord of
the Rings* is what Tolkien called 'the half republic half aris-
tocracy of the Shire',[33] which in fact hardly has a Government

at all. Whilst of course the victory of the West lies in, as the title of the last volume of *The Lord of the Rings* says, not a 'world made safe for democracy' but 'the return of the King'. Clearly Tolkien, as he himself said, was not 'a "democrat" in any of its current uses'.[34] Yet Aragorn, King Elessar, is no tyrant or Duce but a wise, benevolent overseer respecting local traditions of self-government and independence. No commissar or gauleiter is sent from Minas Tirith to govern the Shire but, on the contrary, the hobbits are left to elect their own Sam Gamgee as Mayor of 'a Free Land under the protection of the Northern Sceptre'.[35]

The Free Peoples of Middle-earth may not live in democracies but then, as Professor Shippey points out, 'freedom is not a prerogative of democracies'.[36] Slavery, however, is a prerogative of over-mighty States, epitomized on Middle-earth by the Dark Lord's totalitarian tyranny, with modern Fascism and Communism, both of which Tolkien abhorred, echoed in Orcs reporting each other's 'name and number to the Nazgûl'.[37] Meanwhile, the ordinary folk of Middle-earth, far from being downtrodden by the Lords of the Free, are the ones to whom the Great and the Wise turn in their hour of need. It is not the royal Aragorn nor the wizard Gandalf but Frodo Baggins, timid Hobbit of the Shire, who is the principal hero of *The Lord of the Rings*.

Middle-earth is also a world of 'less noise and more green', in which, for example, forests and trees are valued in themselves, not as 'resources of timber'. His biographer reveals that Tolkien refused to drive a car once he saw the harm they did to the countryside and, even when a wealthy man from the royalties received from worldwide sales of his books, had neither television, dishwasher nor washing machine in his house.[38] Tolkien's is a world in which honour and decency count for far more than material wealth, and in which it is through materialistic greed, possessiveness and lust for temporal power that the One Ring wreaks its ill.

The anti-materialist 'manifesto' implicit in *The Lord of the Rings* has met with predictable politically correct knee-jerkings. One American college professor complained that 'If we attempt to transfer the moral values inherent in the trilogy to the "real world" we find that they may be entitled paternalistic, reactionary, racist, fascistic, and, perhaps worst of all in contemporary terms, irrelevant.'[39] Ironically, the same anthology of Tolkien criticism which includes this outburst also boasts a paper by another US academic praising Tolkien for his 'anti-fascism'![40]

The latter is nearer the truth. Tolkien's view of fascism emerges from a letter to his son Michael in 1941: 'I have in this War a burning private grudge ... against that ruddy little ignoramus Adolf Hitler [for] ruining, perverting, misapplying and making for ever accursed, that noble Northern spirit, a supreme contribution to Europe, which I have ever loved, and tried to present in its true light.'[41] More revealing of Tolkien's actual political viewpoint is yet another of his wartime letters to his son Christopher:

> My political opinions lean more and more to Anarchy (philosophically understood, meaning abolition of control not whiskered men with bombs) – or to 'unconstitutional' Monarchy. I would arrest anyone who uses the word State (in any sense other than the inanimate realm of England and its inhabitants, a thing that has neither power, rights nor mind) ... the proper study of Man is anything but Man; and the most improper job of any man, even saints (who at any rate were at least unwilling to take it on) is bossing other men. Not one in a million is fit for it, and least of all those who seek the opportunity ... the special horror of the present world is that the whole damned thing is in one bag. There is nowhere to fly to. Even the unlucky little Samoyedes, I suspect, have tinned food and the village loudspeaker telling Stalin's bed-time stories about

Democracy and the wicked Fascists who eat babies and steal sledge-dogs ...[42]

Perhaps Tolkien's position is summed up as well as any by Professor Shippey who wrote that 'English tradition' was at the centre of everything he wrote:

Tolkien was prepared to accept connections by blood with Iceland or Saxony or America and (in a more gingerly way) by old proximity with the Irish or even the Finns. However, he was in some ways what would now be called an 'ethnic' writer, though the rule for 'ethnicity' seems to be that anyone can have it *except* Anglo-Saxons (Tolkien was not quite a WASP). Largely this restriction is a penalty of success; since English is international the language naturally ceases to carry strong national sentiment. Behind that success, though, Tolkien was conscious of many centuries of discouragement which had suppressed native tradition in England more quickly, perhaps, than in any other European country. He valued what was left the more highly. In much of what he wrote and read one can see him trying to return to the time before the confusion set in, when the traditions of the Shire and the Mark were uncorrupted.[43]

One wonders whether Professor Shippey's analysis holds the key to Tolkien's phenomenal success.

Is this why Tolkien seems to speak for millions in our corrupt, confused modern world? Is this why Tolkien's implicit assertion of cultural identity, his 'mythology for England' and the glimpse of a world whose values are the antithesis of modern 'Americo-cosmopolitanism' strikes so widespread and enduring a chord in so many hearts? Does Tolkien's rejection of our debased consumer society reflect a similar rejection on the part of his readers? Does it show that in the midst of the Shadow of our modern Mordor there is still hope?

Perhaps our Shadow, like Sauron's, will be 'only a small and passing thing'. Perhaps Tolkien has shown that beyond the modern anti-culture, there is 'light and high beauty for ever beyond its reach'.

> *From the ashes a fire shall be woken,*
> *A light from the shadows shall spring;*
> *Renewed shall be blade that was broken,*
> *The crownless again shall be king!*

NOTES

1. Humphrey Carpenter (ed.), *The Letters of J. R. R. Tolkien*, London: Allen & Unwin, 1981, p. 218.

2. Ibid., p. 212.

3. Ibid., p. 108.

4. Ibid., p. 54.

5. Ibid., p. 65.

6. Ibid., p. 239.

7. J. R. R. Tolkien, *The Lord of the Rings*, London: Allen & Unwin, second edn., 1966, Vol. 1, p. 11.

8. Carpenter, *The Letters of J. R. R. Tolkien*, p. 250.

9. Ibid., p. 230.

10. Ibid., p. 288.

11. Ibid., p. 360.

12. J. R. R. Tolkien, 'Guide to the Names in *The Lord of the Rings*', published in Jared Lobdell (ed.), *A Tolkien Compass*, New York: Ballantine, 1980, p. 171.

13. Humphrey Carpenter, *J. R. R. Tolkien: A Biography*, London: Allen & Unwin, 1977, p. 176.

14. Ibid., p. 81.

15. Carpenter, *The Letters of J. R. R. Tolkien*, p. 88.

16. Ibid., p. 26.

17. T. A. Shippey, *The Road to Middle-Earth*, London: Allen & Unwin, 1982, p. 94.

18. Carpenter, *The Letters of J. R. R. Tolkien*, p. 119.

19. Ibid., p. 212.

20. Paul H. Kocher, *A Reader's Guide to The Silmarillion*, London: Thames & Hudson, 1980, p. 1.

21. Carpenter, *Tolkien: A Biography*, p. 59.

22. Carpenter, *The Letters of J. R. R. Tolkien*, p. 144.

23. Shippey, *The Road to Middle-earth*, p. 181.

24. Carpenter, *Tolkien: A Biography*, p. 129.

25. Carpenter, *The Letters of J. R. R. Tolkien*, p. 145.

26. Ibid., p. 64.

27. Ibid., p. 65.

28. Alida Becker (ed.), *The Tolkien Scrapbook*, Philadelphia: Running Press, 1978, p. 26.

29. Ibid., p. 86.

30. Paul H. Kocher, *Master of Middle-earth: The Achievement of J. R. R. Tolkien*, London: Thames & Hudson, 1973, pp. 127–8.

31. Shippey, *The Road to Middle-earth*, p. 185.

32. Lobdell, *A Tolkien Compass*, p. 52.

33. Carpenter, *The Letters of J. R. R. Tolkien*, p. 241.

34. Ibid., p. 215.

35. Tolkien, *The Lord of the Rings*, Vol. 3, App. B, p. 377.

36. Shippey, *The Road to Middle-earth*, p. 95.

37. Tolkien, *The Lord of the Rings*, Vol. 3, p. 203.

38. Carpenter, *Tolkien: A Biography*, pp. 159, 205.

39. Lobdell, *A Tolkien Compass*, p. 54.

40. Ibid., p. 116.

41. Carpenter, *The Letters of J. R. R. Tolkien*, p. 55.

42. Ibid., pp. 63–4.

43. Shippey, *The Road to Middle-earth*, p. 226.

8

The Sense of Time in Tolkien's The Lord of the Rings

Kevin Aldrich

This article first appeared in the Autumn 1988 edition of Mythlore.

J. R. R. Tolkien's *The Lord of the Rings* is a deeply religious work despite the almost complete lack of reference to the sacred. Tolkien was a Roman Catholic and the mythology behind *The Lord of the Rings* is consonant with the book of Genesis and Roman Catholic moral theology. Indeed, Tolkien's moral vision is essentially the Roman Catholic moral vision, though the colouring in which it is seen is Tolkien's own. This is not to say that the story was consciously meant to be didactic or allegorical. Quite the contrary. It is a story which exists for itself, one which contains and out of which shines certain religious and moral truths.

This was Tolkien's own view. At the end of a letter dated 14 October 1958 to Rhona Beare, he said:

> Theologically (if the term is not too grandiose) I imagine the picture [of reality in Middle-earth] to be less dissonant from what some (including myself) believe to be the truth. But since I have deliberately written a tale, which is built on or out of certain 'religious' ideas, but is *not* an allegory of them (or anything else), and does not mention them overtly, still less preach them, I will not now depart from that mode, and venture on theological disquisition for

which I am not fitted. But I might say that if the tale is 'about' anything (other than itself), it is not as seems widely supposed about 'power'. Power-seeking is only the motive-power that sets events going and is relatively unimportant, I think. It is mainly concerned with Death and Immortality; and the 'escapes': serial longevity, and hoarding memory. (*Let*:283–4)[1]

What Tolkien is saying is that he believes that the picture of reality presented in *The Lord of the Rings* is consonant with the vision of reality in Christianity. *The Lord of the Rings*, in his view, is not about power, but really has to do with 'Death and Immortality' and escaping from death or trying to, which in the story is a foolish and wicked thing to attempt. Much of the poignancy at the end of *The Lord of the Rings* arises from our sense of the inevitable passing of time which sweeps away everything. Perhaps the most powerful temptation for both men and Elves in Tolkien's world – and one which touches us because it reaches to the depths of our being – is to deal with death and time on their own terms rather than the Creator's. Drawing upon both *The Lord of the Rings* and some of the myths behind Tolkien's romance, my aim will be to explore, though certainly not exhaustively, the way men and Elves respond to the mystery of Time, a mystery of our own lives.

What may seem to be a ridiculous question, but on second thought I think is not, is: Does *The Lord of the Rings* have a happy ending? Indeed, there is the joy of the victory over evil in 'The Field of Cormallen' (Chapter 4 of Book Six) in which Sam asks Gandalf, 'Is everything sad going to come untrue?' (III:230).[2] There are the marriages of Faramir and Éowyn, Aragorn and Arwen, and later, Samwise and Rosie. There is the restoration of Gondor and of the Shire. Yet my feeling is that the main note that the book leaves us with is one of poignancy, in which sorrow overpowers joy.

This can be seen in the denouement of *The Lord of the Rings*, which lasts roughly six chapters. It begins after the destruction of the Ring in the chapter called 'Mount Doom' (Chapter 3 of Book Six), at the end of which Frodo says to Sam, 'I am glad you are here with me. Here at the end of all things, Sam' (III:225). It ends when we stand with Sam at the Grey Havens watching those we love most, Frodo, Gandalf, Galadriel – among others – sailing off to Valinor, to a place of happiness, healing and (apparently) immortality, while we are left behind with Sam in the 'real' world, subject to every sorrow and finally death.[3]

And so the joy of the 'eucatastrophe' of the destruction of the Ring and of Sauron, of evil, the 'good turning' in which the Quest succeeds beyond all hope bringing with it great joy, gives way in the denouement to sadness.[4] The world Sam returned to after Frodo and Gandalf departed, according to Tolkien's fiction, has since been totally swept away by time with no trace remaining, just as our world and we ourselves will one day be lost. A line from an Old English poem Tolkien the medieval scholar was certainly aware of called 'Widsith' epitomizes what some might call the gloomy but realistic pagan 'Germanic' view of life: 'Till all things vanish, light and life/Passing together'.[5] Or consider the Anglo-Saxon poem 'The Wanderer' in which the sage concludes his lament,

> Here wealth is fleeting, friends are fleeting,
> Man is fleeting, maid is fleeting;
> All the foundation of earth shall fail![6]

This seeming pessimism in both *The Lord of the Rings* and Old English literature has led at least two critics to conclude that *The Lord of the Rings* is a 'Germanic' work. C. Stuart Hannabuss sees in *The Lord of the Rings* a 'working out of a quasi-Christian morality in pagan terms' in which the ultimate victory goes to the good. Yet, he says, 'the victory over bad is almost Pyrrhic: so clearly do the heroes anticipate and acknowledge defeat that we are in the world of *Beowulf* and the Norse sagas'.[7] Similar to Hannabuss' theory is that of Patricia Meyer Spacks. Claiming that *The Lord of the Rings* is 'by no means a Christian work' (though admitting that the hero grows in specifically Christian virtues, that free will is exercised and there is the possibility of grace, and that Tolkien's universe, unlike the Anglo-Saxons', is ultimately affirmative), Spacks views the book as a northern heroic myth which takes a dark view of life. 'The Anglo-Saxon epic hero operates under the shadow of fate; his struggle is doomed to final failure – the dragon at last, in some encounter, will win.'[8] Tolkien's remarks in his classic essay 'Beowulf: The Monsters and the Critics', are the best I have seen on the 'Germanic' vision, but he considered *Beowulf*'s author to be a Christian who was looking back at a heathen-heroic past, and his theme, 'man at war with the hostile world, and his inevitable overthrow in Time' is one 'no Christian need despise'.[9]

A good place to begin an examination of the theme of death and immortality is the Ring Rhyme that begins each of the volumes of *The Lord of the Rings*. I'd like to focus on the first three lines:

> Three Rings for the Elven-kings under the sky,
> Seven for the Dwarf-lords in their halls of stone,
> Nine for Mortal Men doomed to die ...

We have here three pithy descriptions of essential characteristics of the three major races of rational beings found in Middle-earth. First are the Elves who are 'under the sky'. The Elves are the first-born of the rational beings on Earth who awoke under the night sky before the sun or moon, whose characteristic stance was walking in the starlight when darkness held no evil. (This, by the way, is how we first meet the Elves in *The Lord of the Rings*, when the Hobbits encounter Gildor. The Elves' singing under the stars rescues the Hobbits from the Black Riders.)

Then there are the Dwarves 'in their halls of stone'. As we think of man created out of dust or clay, the Dwarves are made of stone (*Sil*:44). They lived most happily under the earth, workers of metals and carvers of elaborately beautiful palaces or 'halls' under the ground.

And finally, how are men presented? We are 'Mortal Men doomed to die'. The heavily stressed alliterative syllables 'Mortal Men' and 'doomed to die' sound ominous. And in the space of six syllables we are told three times of man's mortality. We are 'mortal', we are 'doomed', and we will 'die'. The main note of man's existence, then, in this apparently simple little poem seems to be his mortality.

Tolkien's mythological origin for man is not difficult to harmonize with Genesis. Tolkien's story of Middle-earth is feigned history: 'The Fall of Man is in the past and off stage; the Redemption of man in the far future' (*Let*:387). The same can be said of his creation, for, in Tolkien's world, all of the early records come from the Elves who are concerned mainly with their own history. According to the Eldar (the first-born Elves),

> Men came into the world in the time of the Shadow of Morgoth and they fell swiftly under his dominion; for he sent his emissaries among them, and they listened to his evil and cunning words, and they worshipped the Darkness and yet feared it. (*Sil*:259)

Some men 'turned from evil' and wandered westward, and because of the aid they gave the Elves in their war against Morgoth, were rewarded by the Valar with many gifts, including the land of Númenor, an Eden-like island near

Valinor, the friendship of the Valar, and a lifespan three times that of normal mortals (*Sil*:259ff.). It was perhaps as close to a heaven-on-earth as men are capable of. The one prohibition placed upon the existence of these men was that they were never to sail west towards the home of the Valar and never to set foot upon that land, for the Valar, they said, had not the authority to remove what was once a 'gift' and is now a 'Doom', death (*Sil*:262 and 265).

As generations passed and the Númenorean culture grew in splendour and power, a discontent began to develop over the fact that they, as mortal men, must leave their joyful lives and all their works behind them, while the Elves and the Valar had unending bliss.

> Why should we not envy the Valar, or even the least of the Deathless [the Elves]? For of us is required a blind trust, and a hope without assurance, knowing not what lies before us in a little while. And yet we also love the Earth and would not lose it. (*Sil*:265)

Later, the Númenoreans were seduced by Melkor's chief servant Sauron, a fallen angelic being. By exploiting the Númenoreans' growing envy of the apparently unending bliss of the Elves and the Valar in Aman (Valinor), Sauron incited them to disobey the prohibition which the Valar had imposed upon them. Part of Sauron's lie was that Melkor, not Eru, was the one true God (*Sil*:271) and that if they would conquer the Blessed Realm they could possess immortality (*Sil*:274–5). Yet they knew that death was Ilúvatar's will for them, against which they should not rebel (*Sil*:264–5). A few Númenoreans who remained faithful to Ilúvatar and the Valar – as one said, 'there is but one loyalty from which no man can be absolved in heart for any cause' (*Sil*:275) – were allowed to escape from the ruin of Númenor and become the rulers of the West of Middle-earth. By the end of the Third

Age, however, it was thought that the line of kings of Númenorean descent had died out (I:257–8).

Aragorn, the last man in whom the blood of Númenor ran true, possesses three preternatural gifts. His longevity is the result of the gift the Valar gave his ancestors. His ability to heal – 'The hands of the king are the hands of a healer' (III:136) – may be the result of the maiarian (angelic) and Elvish strain in the line of Elros (*Sil*:306) or it too may be the Valar's gift.

As a Númenorean, Aragorn also possesses the gift of dying voluntarily, not suicide but surrendering his life when the end is approaching (III:343–4). Tolkien thought this was a gift that unfallen man might have possessed.

> It was also the Elvish (an uncorrupted Númenorean) view that a 'good' Man would or should *die* voluntarily by surrender with trust before being compelled (as did Aragorn). This may have been the nature of *unfallen* Man; though *compulsion* would not threaten him: he would desire and ask to be allowed to 'go on' to a higher state. The Assumption of Mary, the only *unfallen* person, may be regarded as in some ways a simple regaining of unfallen grace and liberty: she asked to be received, and was, having no further function on Earth. (Note to *Let*:286, his italics)

Of course Aragorn's gift is not an assumption of body and soul together into heaven but rather a willing separation of them. He could give back the gift of longevity he had been given and not without hope. When he is about to lay down his life and his half-Elven wife Arwen is in despair, he says, 'Behold! we are not bound for ever to the circles of the world, and beyond them is more than memory' (III:344).

Each of Aragorn's gifts, it may be noticed, has to do with man's mortality – with increasing life's length, restoring health, and finally, accepting death.

In direct contrast to mortal men are the Elves, who enjoy a seeming immortality, which is actually a special kind of longevity. The Elves' fate is in a way like the Valar's. The Valar are angelic spiritual beings who at Eru's invitation chose to enter into the world and take part in its shaping:

> But this condition Ilúvatar made, or it is the necessity of their love, that their power should thenceforward be contained and bounded in the World, to be within it forever, until it is complete, so that they are its life and it is theirs. And therefore they are named the Valar, the Powers of the World. (*Sil*:20)

The Valar are bound to the world as long as it lasts. Similarly, the Elves do not die until the world dies:

> the Elves remain until the end of days, and their love of the Earth and all the world is more single and more poignant therefore, and as the years lengthen ever more sorrowful. For the Elves die not till the world dies, unless they are slain or waste in grief (and to both these seeming deaths they are subject); neither does age subdue their strength, unless one grow weary of ten thousand centuries; and dying they are gathered to the halls of Mandos in Valinor, whence they may in time return. (*Sil*:42)

The Elves' sadness arises out of love for their lands and works which cannot be held on to because of the ravages of time, whether through natural changes or the injuries of their enemies. For this reason, as Galadriel says, 'their regret is undying and cannot ever wholly be assuaged' (I:380). The desire to halt the passage of time was one of the motives behind the forging of the Three Elven Rings. As Elrond says, those who made them desired 'understanding, making, and healing, to preserve all things unstained' (I:282, cf. *Sil*:288).

Galadriel had achieved this in Lothlórien. After the Travellers' blindfolds were removed and they beheld the mound of Amroth,

> Frodo stood awhile lost in wonder. It seemed to him that he stepped through a high window that looked on a vanished world. A light was upon it for which his language had no name. All that he saw was shapely, but the shapes seemed at once clear cut, as if they had been first conceived and drawn at the uncovering of his eyes and ancient as if they had endured for ever. He saw no colour but those he knew, gold and white and blue and green, but they were fresh and poignant, as if he had at that moment first perceived them and made for them names new and wonderful. In winter here no heart could mourn for summer or for spring. No blemish or sickness or deformity could be seen in anything that grew upon the earth. On the land of Lórien there was no stain. (I:365)

Lórien is a sanctuary in the midst of the transient world where not only is there no evil, but time itself appears to be halted. It is as if the garden Frodo is in is the garden of Eden before the Fall, and Frodo is like Adam beholding the splendour of creation with the power to name creatures: 'and whatever the man called each living creature, that was its name' (Genesis 2:19).

But while from our mortal point of view what the Elves have done in Lothlórien seems utterly wonderful, Tolkien saw a darker side to both their presence in Middle-earth and their attempts to halt time.

> They wanted the peace and bliss and perfect memory of 'The West' [Valinor], and yet to remain on the ordinary earth where their prestige as the highest people, above wild Elves, Dwarves, and Men, was greater than at the

bottom of the hierarchy of Valinor. They thus became obsessed with 'fading', the mode in which the changes of time (the law of the world under the sun) was perceived by them. They became sad, and their art (shall we say) anti-quarian, and their efforts all really a kind of embalming – even though they also retained the old motive of their kind, the adornment of earth, and the healing of its hurts. (*Let*:151–2)

Tolkien saw an element of pride in the Elves, an unwilling-ness to be just Elves, not Valar or 'gods'. It is at first, perhaps, hard for us to see why they would not gladly accept the place assigned to them in the world, since from our point of view to be an Elf in Valinor seems a more excellent fate than to be a mortal man. But then to an Elf, of course, it could seem better to be a Valar than a mere Elf. The problem is the same as Adam's. Why would he, considering all the gifts he was given by God, still rather be a 'god'? Or, why would Morgoth or Satan want to usurp God's place?

At any rate, while there is nothing wrong with the Elves' 'old motive' of adorning the earth and healing its hurts, they perceive change itself as an evil. This is wrong because change or 'the law of the world' is Eru's will. Further, it is Eru's will that the Elves should 'fade', that is, become less and less important in the affairs of Middle-earth, and go to the West. Finally, behind their desire to halt time is perhaps also an unwillingness to accept their own mortality, since time will eventually bring about their end. Yet the Elves of Middle-earth have not fallen; they haven't directly rebelled against Eru's will. Rather, they have been prolonging their days in Middle-earth as long as possible.

By the end of the Third Age the Elves can no longer put off whether they will accept or reject Eru's will for them. Should Sauron regain the One Ring he will destroy all their works; and even if the One is destroyed, the Three will lose their power and the 'tides of Time will sweep' their works away (I:380). The Elves choose to give up Middle-earth for the Blessed Realm. Galadriel, who has desired the Ring, rejects it and will not try to become a goddess, 'beautiful and terrible as the Morning and the Night! Fair as the Sea and the Sun and the Snow upon the Mountain! Dreadful as the Storm and the Lightning! Stronger than the foundations of the earth' (I:381). Instead she will remain just herself: 'I will diminish, and go into the West, and remain Galadriel' (I:381). Again it is hard for 'Mortal Men doomed to die' to understand the sorrow and regret of the Elves, since they will be going to a kind of natural paradise. But though we admire and envy the lifespan of the Elves, it is nevertheless finite, and as the world comes to its end, they will come to theirs: they apparently will die utterly, though 'Ilúvatar has not revealed what he purposes for the Elves after the World's end' (*Sil*:42).

On the other hand, Ilúvatar gave to men what are in the Elves' opinion 'strange gifts' (*Sil*:41). Eru 'willed that the hearts of Man should seek beyond the world and should find no rest therein' (*Sil*:41). He also willed that they would

> have a virtue to shape their life, amid the powers and chances of the world, beyond the Music of the Ainur, which is fate to all things else; and of their operation everything should be, in form and deed, completed, and the world fulfilled unto the last and smallest. (*Sil*:41–2)

I am not sure what the first part of this statement means – not, I think, that men possess free will and Elves don't, since Galadriel obviously does. Perhaps it means that men alone of all earthly creatures are supernatural. The Elves are natural, bound to the world, while men are meant to leave it. The second part, that the world – the earth, not the universe – should be fulfilled through them, seems to be the biblical notion that the earth is made for man: 'Be fruitful and increase, fill the earth and subdue it, rule over the fish of the sea, the birds of heaven, and every living thing that moves upon the earth' (Genesis 1:28). As Aulë says to Yavanna,

> Eru will give them [his 'Children'] dominion, and they shall use all that they find in Arda: though not, by the purpose of Eru, without respect or without gratitude. (*Sil*:45)

To this Yavanna replies, 'Not unless Melkor darken their hearts' (*Sil*:45). Though in this context the Children who will have dominion include the Elves (and Dwarves) as well as men, Aulë's statement seems to apply pre-eminently to the latter, because eventually all the peoples except man die or leave the circles of this world.

But, according to the Eldar, Ilúvatar knew that men, 'being set amid the turmoils of the powers of the world, would stray often, and would not use their gifts in harmony' (*Sil*:42). To this he said, as he said in regard to Melkor's evil, 'These too in their time shall find that all that they do redounds at the end only to the glory of my work' (*Sil*:42).

Consonant with this 'gift of freedom', whether from purely natural ends or to dominate their environment, men live only a short while. Men truly die (as Elves only seem to) and leave the world, and so the Elves call them the 'Guests' or 'Strangers' (*Sil*:42).

> Death is their fate, the gift of Ilúvatar, which as Time wears even the Powers shall envy. But Melkor has cast his shadow upon it, and confounded it with darkness, and brought evil out of good and fear out of hope. (*Sil*:42)

In Tolkien's mythology death is not seen as a punishment but a gift given by God. Of course many of the men in his world see it as a curse, as we saw with the Númenoreans. Is this view of death as a gift in contradiction to the Catholic one? Tolkien didn't think so. The idea of death as a gift is 'an Elvish perception of what *death* – not being tied to the "circles of the world" – should now become for Men, however it arose' (*Let*:286). It

> does not necessarily have anything to say for or against such beliefs as the Christian that 'death' is not part of human nature, but a punishment for sin (rebellion), a result of the 'Fall'. A divine 'punishment' is also a divine 'gift', if accepted, since its object is ultimate blessing, and the supreme inventiveness of the Creator will make 'punishments' (that is changes of design) produce a good not otherwise to be attained: a 'mortal' Man has probably (an Elf would say) a higher if unrevealed destiny than a longeval one. To attempt by device or 'magic' to recover longevity is thus a supreme folly and wickedness of 'mortals'. Longevity or counterfeit 'immortality' (true immortality is beyond Eä) is the chief bait of Sauron – it leads the small to a Gollum, and the great to a Ringwraith. (*Let*:285–6)

For both Elves and men, then, time is perceived as an enemy. The Rings of Power are all, at least in part, anti-time devices. The Three, which were untainted by Sauron, are 'good' so far as the Elves' desire to 'preserve all things unstained' is good. The Nine and the One offered an apparent immortality to mortals but that promise was a lie: Sauron designed these weapons simply to enslave his enemies.

The problem of death and change remains after the Ring is destroyed. Even when the great objective evil is removed, when man and hobbit are able to live the good life – in Minas Tirith or the Shire – time continues to wear away. As mentioned at the beginning of this essay, at the end of *The Lord of the Rings* we are left standing on the shores of mortal lands watching those we love sailing away into immortality, escaping, we think, from time. We couldn't know from the rest of *The Lord of the Rings* that Frodo and Bilbo would eventually have to die (*Let*:328) and that even for the Elves time is growing short – even ten thousand centuries will have an end. And for those left behind, however great the bliss, life must end:

> I say to you, King of the Númenoreans, not till now have I understood the tale of your people and their fall. As wicked fools I scorned them, but I pity them at last. For if this is indeed, as the Eldar say, the gift of the One to Men, it is bitter to receive. (III:344)

Those are the words of Arwen the half-Elven who chose mortality to marry Aragorn. As bitter as it is to receive, death is just what a mortal man, or woman, should willingly accept from the Creator. In the last episode of *The Lord of the Rings* which we can read, the cold and grey figure of Arwen returns to the now empty land of Lórien and amid the falling leaves lays down her life:

> and there in her green grave, until the world is changed, and all the days of her life are utterly forgotten by men that come after, and elanor and niphredil bloom no more east of the Sea. (III:344)

Spacks is partly correct: man will be overthrown in Time, but then so will everything else – evil, the Elves, the world itself. But man will arise, Aragorn hopes, as Tolkien hoped. Death will not win. There is more beyond the circles of the world than 'memory', that is, the memory Arwen would possess of her life with Aragorn if she abandoned Middle-earth and mortality and went to the West (III:343–4). For, as the Valar declared to the Eldar, men will join the Second Music of the

Ainur (*Sil*:42) in which 'the themes of Ilúvatar shall be played aright' (*Sil*:15).

For both men and Elves, 'good' means being the kind of creatures Eru wills that they be. At the end of the Third Age, the Elves had the potential for a great fall, but they chose rather to 'fade'. For *mortal* men, good means accepting their mortality. It seems to Gimli the Dwarf that men 'come to naught in the end but might-have-beens' (III:149), and the Númenoreans who envied the Valar complained that 'of us is required a blind trust, and a hope without assurance' (*Sil*:265). *The Lord of the Rings* is about immortality and escape from death. But there is no escape *from* death except *through* death, if at all. The Gift of the One to men is bitter to receive, as Arwen says, but there is hope 'beyond the circles of the world'. What *The Lord of the Rings* has to say ultimately is that if true happiness is to be found by mortals, it will be found not in time but in eternity. *The Lord of the Rings*' author has passed into eternity. And so shall we all.

NOTES

1. All citations from Tolkien's letters are from Humphrey Carpenter (ed.), *The Letters of J. R. R. Tolkien*, Boston: Houghton Mifflin Co., 1981, and will be indicated by the abbreviation *Let* followed by the page number.

2. All textual citations from *The Lord of the Rings* are from the Second Edition, Boston: Houghton Mifflin Co., 1965, and give the volume number in roman numerals followed by the page numbers in arabic numerals.

3. For readers not familiar with Tolkien's mythology, perhaps a recap of his creation myth 'The Music of the Ainur' might be useful. Eru or Ilúvatar or the One is the monotheistic god of Eä, the created material universe. The Ainur are his first beings, the angels. The Music of the Ainur is a sort of huge symphony made by Ilúvatar and

all the Ainur (both those who would remain good and those who will fall), which Ilúvatar then showed to them in a vision. He then spoke the word 'Eä' meaning 'Let these things Be!' (*Sil*:20) and the universe began. The Valar are the good angelic beings who are the co-creators and guardians of Arda, the earth. Some of them are Aulë, Yavanna, and Elbereth. Valinor is the natural paradise where they dwell. Morgoth, like Sauron his underling, is a fallen angelic being who tried to conquer and ruin the world.

4. For Tolkien's discussion of the purpose of fairy tales see 'On Fairy-Stories', published as part of *Tree and Leaf* in *The Tolkien Reader*, New York: Ballantine, 1966.

5. *An Anthology of Old English Poetry*, Translated by Charles W. Kennedy, New York: Oxford University Press, 1960, p. 61.

6. Ibid., p. 7.

7. C. Stuart Hannabuss, 'Deep Down', *Signal*, September 1971, pp. 87–8. Quoted from Dedria Bryfonske (ed.), *Contemporary Literary Criticism*, Vol. 12, Detroit: Gale Research, 1981, p. 575.

8. Patricia Meyer Spacks, 'Power and Meaning in *The Lord of the Rings*', from Neil D. Isaacs and Rose A. Zimbardo (eds.), *Tolkien and the Critics*, Notre Dame: Notre Dame University Press, 1968, pp. 82–94.

9. J. R. R. Tolkien, 'Beowulf: The Monsters and the Critics', from Lewis E. Nicholson (ed.), *An Anthology of Beowulf Criticism*, Notre Dame: Notre Dame University Press, 1963, pp. 51–103. Originally delivered as the Sir Israel Gollancz Memorial Lecture of 1936 and published in the *Proceedings of the British Academy*, 22, 1936, pp. 245–95. My quotes are from Nicholson, pp. 67 and 73.

9

TOLKIEN AND THE CATHOLIC LITERARY REVIVAL
JOSEPH PEARCE

Joseph Pearce is the author of Tolkien: Man and Myth *and* Wisdom and Innocence: A Life of G. K. Chesterton. *His first novel,* The Three Ys Men, *is, according to his own estimation, 'a rumbustious romp in the tradition of Belloc and Chesterton with just a hint of Tolkien's lighter fiction'. He is a full-time writer living in Norfolk.*

If one were asked to list the key Catholic literary figures of the twentieth century, it is likely that the names of Chesterton, Belloc, Waugh and Greene would spring to mind. It is equally likely that the name of Tolkien would be overlooked. The author of *The Lord of the Rings* is not generally perceived to be one of the key protagonists of the Catholic literary revival, a fact which reflects the extent to which his work is misunderstood. Tolkien's Christian faith is often ignored by critics or else, when alluded to, is dismissed as an aberration which had little or no effect on his sub-creation. There is in fact an amusing irony in the parallel between Tolkien's position and that of Graham Greene. During the course of his last interview, Greene had reiterated his oft-repeated disclaimer that he was 'not a Catholic writer' but 'a writer who happens to be a Catholic'.[1] Yet in spite of his protestations to the contrary Greene's novels are still considered intrinsically to be those of a Catholic writer. On the other hand, if Tolkien had ever made the claim that he was not a Catholic writer few would have questioned its validity.

The Lord of the Rings and *The Silmarillion* are not in any sense 'Christian', it is claimed, merely the work of someone 'who happens to be a Catholic'.

The problem arises when one realizes that Tolkien's own view of the relationship of his faith to his art was almost diametrically opposed to that espoused by Greene. For Tolkien, his faith was of paramount importance and absolutely essential to his sub-creation. In a letter to a friend he stated that '*The Lord of the Rings* is of course a fundamentally religious and Catholic work; unconsciously so at first, but consciously in the revision.'[2] Similarly, George Sayer, another friend, has remarked that '*The Lord of the Rings* would have been very different, and the writing of it very difficult, if Tolkien hadn't been a Christian. He thought it a profoundly Christian book.'[3] Tolkien was also pleased when Father Robert Murray had written to say that the book had left him with a strong sense of 'a positive compatibility with the order of Grace' and that the image of Galadriel was reminiscent of the Virgin Mary. 'I have been cheered specially by what you have said,' Tolkien replied, 'because you are more perceptive, especially in some directions, than anyone else, and have even revealed to me more clearly some things about my work. I think I know exactly what you mean by the order of Grace; and of course by your references to Our Lady, upon which all my own small perception of beauty both in majesty and simplicity is founded.'[4]

Following his assertion that *The Lord of the Rings* was 'fundamentally religious and Catholic', Tolkien had added that he was 'grateful for having been brought up (since I was eight) in a Faith that has nourished me and taught me all the little that I know; and that I owe to my mother, who clung to her conversion and died young, largely through the hardships of poverty resulting from it'.[5]

On another occasion Tolkien sought to emphasize the importance of his faith in less emotive language, placing it at the pinnacle of a hierarchy of influences which he called the 'scale of significance':

> I object to the contemporary trend in criticism, with its excessive interest in the details of the lives of authors and artists. They only distract attention from an author's work . . . and end, as one now often sees, in becoming the main interest. But only one's guardian Angel, or indeed God Himself, could unravel the real relationship between personal facts and an author's works. Not the author himself (though he knows more than any investigator), and certainly not so-called 'psychologists'.
>
> But, of course, there is a scale of significance in 'facts' of this sort.[6]

Tolkien then divided the 'facts' of his own life into three distinct categories, namely the 'insignificant', the 'more significant' and the 'really significant':

> There are insignificant facts (those particularly dear to analysts and writers about writers); such as drunkenness, wife-beating, and suchlike disorders. I do not happen to be guilty of these particular sins. But if I were, I should not suppose that artistic work proceeded from the weaknesses that produced them, but from other and still uncorrupted regions of my being. Modern 'researchers' inform me that Beethoven cheated his publishers, and abominably ill-treated his nephew; but I do not believe that has anything to do with his music.[7]

Apart from these 'insignificant facts', Tolkien believed that there were 'more significant facts, which have some relation to an author's works'. In this category he placed his academic vocation as a philologist. This had affected his 'taste in languages' which was 'obviously a large ingredient in *The*

Lord of the Rings'. Yet even this was subservient to more important factors:

> And there are a few basic facts, which however drily expressed, are really significant. For instance I was born in 1892 and lived for my early years in 'the Shire' in a pre-mechanical age. Or more important, I am a Christian (which can be deduced from my stories), and in fact a Roman Catholic.[8]

Considering Tolkien's insistence on the primary importance to his work of his Christian faith, it is pertinent to place him among the *illustrissimi* of the Catholic literary revival and to look more closely at his place in its historical development.

The revival itself was instigated by John Henry Newman and its beginnings can be said to coincide with Newman's reception into the Church in 1845. The critic George Levine described Newman as 'perhaps the most artful and brilliant prose writer of the nineteenth century'[9] and there is no doubt that his literary achievement was both prodigious and prolific. His works of fiction, *Loss and Gain* and *Callista*, are among the greatest novels of the Victorian era, and his auto-biographical *Apologia* is probably the finest exposition of a religious conversion ever written in the English language. His verse, the most accomplished and most beautiful of which is *The Dream of Gerontius*, places him in the first rank of Victorian poets and, to cap it all, he is considered a popular theologian of rare distinction who warrants a place among the foremost doctors of the Church. Almost single-handedly Newman's genius had revitalized English Catholicism and the quality of his literary output had set the standard that future generations of Catholic writers would seek to emulate.

The greatness of Newman's spirit was to prove a potent influence on Tolkien's early development. From 1902, when he was ten years old, a considerable part of Tolkien's life revolved around the Birmingham Oratory, a large church served by a community of priests which had been established by Newman in 1849. Newman spent the last four decades of his life within the Oratory walls, dying there in 1890. In 1902 the community still included many priests who remembered Newman as a friend and who had served under him, one of whom was Father Francis Xavier Morgan, destined to become Tolkien's guardian following the death of Tolkien's mother two years later.

If Newman's indirect influence on Tolkien's early life is beyond question, the extent of his influence on Tolkien's work is not so easy to verify. The substantial body of Newman's literary output might seem to have little in common with the fantasy genre in which Tolkien excelled. This, however, should not obscure the underlying affinity which exists between the two writers. The difference was not in what they were trying to say but only in the way they were trying to say it. Perhaps the similarity of intention can be seen most clearly in the purgatorial peripatetics employed by both writers. Tolkien's theme in his short story *Leaf by Niggle* and his poem 'Mythopoeia' is not that dissimilar from Newman's vision of the after-life in *The Dream of Gerontius*. Yet these surface similarities are merely a reflection of a deeper unity which springs from the Catholicism which animates their work. For Tolkien and Newman alike, the substantial body of their work is 'Catholic' in so far as it represents an orthodox Christian response to the cynicism and materialism of the age. Both men accepted the former as the only logical alternative to the latter, a view expressed with characteristic eloquence by Newman:

> Turn away from the Catholic Church, and to whom will you go? it is your only chance of peace and assurance in this turbulent, changing world. There is nothing between

it and scepticism, when men exert their reason freely. Private creeds, fancy religions, may be showy and imposing to the many in their day; national religions may lie huge and lifeless, and cumber the ground for centuries, and distract the attention or confuse the judgment of the learned; but on the long run it will be found that either the Catholic Religion is verily and indeed the coming in of the unseen world into this, or that there is nothing positive, nothing dogmatic, nothing real in any one of our notions as to whence we come and whither we are going. Unlearn Catholicism, and you become Protestant, Unitarian, Deist, Pantheist, Sceptic, in a dreadful, but infallible succession . . .[10]

There is much in this short extract from one of Newman's sermons that throws light on Tolkien's sub-creation of Middle-earth. Newman's description of the Catholic religion as 'verily and indeed the coming in of the unseen world into this', offers a key to understanding the hidden forces which give so much depth to *The Lord of the Rings* and *The Silmarillion*. It is the constant awareness of the powers of the unseen world, hidden but real, that fires the imagination and gives these books the creative tension which permeates each page. The other key is Newman's insistence on the stark dichotomy between the Church and the Alternative. There is no murky centre ground between the two, it is a fight between the forces of darkness and the forces of light, between orthodoxy and scepticism. One is reminded of Chesterton's words on his death-bed: 'The issue is now quite clear. It is between light and darkness and everyone must choose his side.'[11]

Neither were the views of Newman, Chesterton or Tolkien the result of an unreasoned religious bigotry. On the contrary, they were anchored in the philosophy of Aristotle and Aquinas and were motivated by a rejection of modern philosophy. The *reductio ad absurdum* which followed on from the 'Enlightenment's' rejection of scholastic philosophy and its espousal of the Cartesian axiom *cogito, ergo sum* was all too obvious. Beginning with 'I think, therefore I am' the modern world had regressed to the ultimate scepticism about the objectivity of existence itself: 'I am but I can't be sure that anything else is.' This regression of modern philosophy from the perennial wisdom of the ancients to the primeval soup of sceptical reductionism was at the heart of Newman's claim that to unlearn Catholicism was to 'become Protestant, Unitarian, Deist, Pantheist, Sceptic, in a dreadful, but infallible succession'.

This philosophical battleground lies at the very core of Tolkien's work and is the ultimate key to its depth and potency. It also explains both its enduring appeal and the continuing hostility it provokes. Those who subscribe, however unwittingly, to the perennial philosophy adopted by the Church will find reassurance in Tolkien's epic tales of the eternal nature of the struggle between good and evil and the moral imperatives and choices which this entails. To the philosophically sceptical, who can't be sure of anything, Tolkien's certainties are merely absurdities. His depths are shallows; his truths are falsehoods; his myths are lies. To tamper with a memorable aphorism of Kipling's, it would seem that light is light and dark is dark and never the twain will meet.

The practical implications of Tolkien's philosophical approach are most evident in his enshrining of the objectivity of truth. Far from his 'fantasy' world representing a flight from reality it is, in the metaphysical sense, a flight into reality. The events in Middle-earth are not merely real, they are hyper-real, too real for comfort, so that the reader is genuinely concerned about the characters and the turn of events, the threat of dyscatastrophe and the joy of eucatastrophe. The ring that Frodo carries is so real that it can't be tossed away and forgotten about. The consequences of doing so would be so disastrous that it would be an unthinkable act. Yet the dangers of not doing so are real also, intensely so, and there is a sublime heroism in the dutiful resolve to bear the burden in spite of the fear and suffering it entails. The ring is not a fantasy, a figment of the mind, an urge, a desire, or an opinion which can be changed, it is a fact which must be faced, borne and finally overcome. This is true realism, built upon the solid rock of objectivism. It has precious little to do with the false realism of the sceptics who base their understanding of reality on the shifting sands of subjectivism where nothing is good, nothing evil, nothing true in itself.

Tolkien's preoccupation with the nature and objectivity of truth leads inevitably back to Newman. In his *Apologia*, his semi-autobiographical novel *Loss and Gain* and his historical novel *Callista*, Newman explored the intricate nature of the individual's quest for truth. In *Callista*, a novel set in the third century, Agellius, a Christian, endeavours in vain to convince his sceptical uncle of the claims of the Church:

> 'O Jucundus,' cried Agellius, irritated at his own inability to express himself or hold an argument, 'if you did but know what it was to have the Truth! The Christian has found the Truth, the eternal Truth, in a world of error. That is his bargain, that is his hire; can there be a greater? Can I give up the Truth? . . .'

His uncle's reply echoed the words of Pilate two centuries previously and those of sceptics many centuries later:

> 'The Truth!' he cried, '*this* is what I understand you to say, – the truth. The *truth* is your bargain; I think I'm right, the truth; Hm; what is truth? What in heaven and earth do you mean by truth? where did you get that cant? What oriental tomfoolery is bamboozling you? The truth!' he cried,

staring at him, half of triumph, half of impatience, 'the truth! Jove help the boy! – the truth! can truth pour me out a cup of melilotus? can truth crown me with flowers? can it sing to me? can it bring Glyceris to me? drop gold in my girdle? or cool my brows when fever visits me? Can truth give me a handsome suburban with some five hundred slaves, or raise me to the duumvirate? Let it do this, and I will worship it; it shall be my god; it shall be more to me than Fortune, Fate, Rome, or any other goddess on the list. But I like to see, and touch, and feel, and handle, and weigh, and measure what is promised me. I wish to have a sample and an instalment. I am too old for chaff. Eat, drink, and be merry, that's my philosophy, that's my religion; and I know no better. Today is ours, tomorrow is our children's.'[12]

In setting this dialogue more than a millennium and a half ago, Newman was emphasizing the perennial nature of the question. Scepticism, hedonism and materialism were not modern inventions but age-old negations, man's continual denial of the truth which eludes him. Neither were they 'progressive'. Throughout history, the accentuation of the negative has led to the decay of civilization and the ultimate return of barbarism. It is symbolized in Christian scripture by Pilate's asking the same question as does Jucundus, coming to the same conclusions, and washing his hands of the whole affair. Pilate, the personification of the eternal sceptic, dismisses truth as unknowable and therefore irrelevant.

In *The Lord of the Rings* and *The Silmarillion* Tolkien uses an invented world for the same reasons that Newman had used the relative distance of antiquity. By placing his epic in Middle-earth he can deal with eternal verities without the distractions of fads, fashions and the flood of ephemera which clutters modern life. If he had set his story in England during the 1940s, he would no doubt have been commended for his 'realism' by contemporary critics, but his 'modern' work would appear dated today and possibly less relevant and real to subsequent generations. Tolkien's sub-created world is timeless, enabling him to ignore the peripheral in favour of the perennial problems of existence. For this reason, *The Lord of the Rings* is no more dated today than it was when it was first published. For the same reason it is safe to predict its continued popularity. If future generations stop reading Tolkien's classic it will not be because it has become irrelevant or dated. Rather, if they stop reading Tolkien it will be because they have stopped reading. If technology makes the written word redundant, Tolkien's work may founder. His books, which have proved too real to be reproduced by any of the new forms of virtual reality, may then be forgotten. If so, it may mark the triumph of technology but certainly not the triumph of 'progress'. In such circumstances one is reminded of the wisdom of Coventry Patmore's poem 'Magna est Veritas':

> Here, in this little Bay,
> Full of tumultuous life and great repose,
> Where, twice a day,
> The purposeless, glad ocean comes and goes,
> Under high cliffs, and far from the huge town,
> I sit me down.
> For want of me the world's course will not fail;
> When all its work is done, the lie shall rot;
> The truth is great, and shall prevail,
> When none cares whether it prevail or not.

This short verse, written by one of the most celebrated Catholic poets of the Victorian era, displays all the hallmarks of the literary revival heralded by Newman. It shows the same preoccupations that characterize the work of both Newman and Tolkien. There is the insistence upon the transcendent and objective nature of truth, and upon its perennial prevalence regardless of the fashionable whims of a largely heedless humanity. More specifically as far as direct comparisons with Tolkien are concerned, there is the same almost mystical reverence for the timeless endurance of the ocean. At the end of *The Lord of the Rings* there is more than a glimmer of the poetic poignancy which Patmore felt in the majestic presence of the sea:

> But to Sam the evening deepened to darkness as he stood at the Haven; and as he looked at the grey sea he saw only a shadow on the waters that was soon lost in the West. There still he stood far into the night, hearing only the sigh and murmur of the waves on the shores of Middle-earth, and the sound of them sank deep into his heart.[13]

This reverence for the sea is given theological expression in *The Silmarillion*:

> And they observed the winds and the air, and the matters of which Arda was made, of iron and stone and silver and gold and many substances: but of all these water they most greatly praised. And it is said by the Eldar that in water there lives yet the echo of the Music of the Ainur more than in any substance else that is in this Earth; and many of the Children of Ilúvatar hearken still unsated to the voices of the Sea, and yet know not for what they listen.[14]

In prose such as this Tolkien succeeds in encapsulating theological principles in terms which are evocative of the metaphysical poets. The Ainur are the angelic powers given responsibility for the Creation of Middle-earth by Ilúvatar, the One omnipotent God. Their collective act of Creation, overseen by the One, is described as the Music, the symphonic sub-creation of the universe. In thus describing water as something in which there still lives the echo of this angelic Music, Tolkien reaches sublime heights of imagery worthy of the great poets.

There is also a striking similarity between the words which Tolkien puts into the mouth of Ulmo, the angel most responsible for the Waters, and the words of the Victorian Catholic poet Francis Thompson in his poem 'To A Snowflake':

> Then Ulmo answered: 'Truly, Water is become now fairer than my heart imagined, neither had my secret thought conceived the snowflake, nor in all my music was contained the falling of the rain . . .'[15]

Compare this with Thompson's verse:

> What heart could have thought you? –
> Past our devisal
> (O filigree petal!)
> Fashioned so purely,
> Fragilely, surely,
> From what Paradisal
> Imagineless metal,
> Too costly for cost?[16]

Unfortunately, modern ignorance of both philosophy and theology has resulted in this deep love of nature being mistaken for a form of pantheistic paganism. The extent to which Tolkien sought to dispel such misunderstanding is evident in the early pages of *The Silmarillion* in which he goes to great pains to ensure that his own version of the Creation myth conforms with orthodox Christianity.

Comparison with another Victorian Catholic poet will illustrate the intrinsic unity which exists between Tolkien's 'greenness' and the Christian philosophy which underpins his work. Gerard Manley Hopkins had been as devastated by the felling of 'ten or twelve' poplar trees in 1879 as had been the young Tolkien by the felling of a favourite tree during his childhood. In both cases the wanton destruction inspired literary creativity. For Hopkins it resulted in the writing of 'Binsey Poplars', one of his finest poems:

> O if we but knew what we do
> > When we delve or hew –
> Hack and rack the growing green!
> > Since country is so tender
> To touch, her being so slender,
> That, like this sleek and seeing ball
> But a prick will make no eye at all,
> Where we, even where we mean
> > To mend her we end her,
> > When we hew or delve:
> After-comers cannot guess the beauty been.
> Ten or twelve, only ten or twelve
> > Strokes of havoc unselve
> > > The sweet especial scene,
> > Rural scene, a rural scene,
> > Sweet especial rural scene.[17]

For Tolkien this love of nature, and especially of trees, bore fruit in his creation of the arboreal ents and in the charming characterization of Treebeard and Quickbeam. As with Hopkins, the roots from which the fruit sprang were philosophical. The creative vision of both men was shaped to a profound extent by the scholastic philosophy of the Church. For Hopkins, the rigours of his training to become a Jesuit left him thoroughly conversant with the philosophy of both Duns Scotus and St Thomas Aquinas. This shaped his notion of *inscape*, the concept at the heart of all his poetry, which was itself a reflection of the teaching of Duns Scotus that everything in creation has a unique spiritual identity, its *haecceitas* or thisness. The concept of inscape also explains the omnipresence of nature-reverence and its mystical significance in Tolkien's work, and this in turn represents a further example of the fact that one must plumb the philosophical depths if one is to understand the colourful surface of Middle-earth.

If comparisons with Newman, Patmore, Thompson and Hopkins illustrate the affinity which exists between Tolkien's work and that of the early protagonists of the Catholic literary revival, comparisons with the works of G. K. Chesterton serve as further evidence that Tolkien's achievement should be seen within the context of an orthodox Christian response to secular society. Like Chesterton, Tolkien subscribed to a vision of Merrie England which was an idealized view of what England had been before the Reformation and what she could be again. It was an England free from post-Reformation Puritanism and post-industrial proletarianism, an England where individuals owned the land on which they lived and worked. It was Blake's green and pleasant land liberated from the dominion of dark, satanic mills. Chesterton had eulogized this mythical England in his verse, his essays and his novels, and Tolkien had sub-created his own version of it with his descriptions of the Shire. 'In many ways,' writes Charles A. Coulombe elsewhere in this volume, 'the Shire expresses perfectly the economic and political ideals of the Church, as expressed by Leo XIII in *Rerum novarum*, and Pius XI in *Quadragesimo anno* . . . It is the sort of society envisioned by Distributists Belloc and Chesterton.'

The linking of the Shire with the Distributism of Chesterton and Belloc moves the discussion of Tolkien's place within the Catholic literary revival from the philosophical to the socio-economic. On this level there are many striking similarities between Chesterton and Tolkien, most notably in their shared distaste for urban industrialism which places them in a long plaintive tradition stretching back to Blake and Cobbett almost two centuries earlier. Chesterton had written a study of Blake and a full-length biography of 'great Cobbett' describing him as 'the horseman of the shires' and the champion of England's dispossessed rural population, the last rustic radical: 'After him Radicalism is urban – and Toryism suburban.'[18] 'In Mr Chesterton's view,' wrote a reviewer, 'Cobbett stood for England: England unindustrialised, self-sufficient, relying on a basis of agriculture and sound commerce for her prosperity, with no desire for inflation.'[19] Chesterton's view of Cobbett's England conforms with Tolkien's view of the Shire which he told his publisher was 'based on rural England and not on any other country in the world'.[20] Comparing Cobbett to Shelley, Chesterton wrote: 'Going through green Warwickshire, Cobbett might have thought of the crops and Shelley of the clouds. But Shelley would have called Birmingham what Cobbett called it – a hell-hole.'[21] This was certainly a view with which Tolkien would have concurred wholeheartedly, especially as he had seen the village in which he had spent his childhood swallowed up during his own lifetime by the 'hell-hole' of the West Midlands conurbation. It is also interesting that Chesterton's description of Cobbett is equally applicable to Tolkien:

> What he saw was not an Eden that cannot exist, but rather an Inferno that can exist, and even that does exist. What he saw was the perishing of the whole English power of self-support, the growth of cities that drain and dry up the countryside ... the toppling triumphs of machines over men ... the wealth that may mean famine and the culture that may mean despair; the bread of Midas and the sword of Damocles.[22]

The evident convergence of opinions raises the question of Chesterton's influence on Tolkien. Chesterton's fame was at its height when Tolkien was still at school and arguably at his most impressionable and it is clear that Tolkien knew, and largely sympathized with, Chesterton's work. Nonetheless, the danger of overstating the case was apparent in Christopher Clausen's essay 'The Lord of the Rings and The Ballad of the White Horse'.[23] Clausen claimed that The Lord of the Rings is 'heavily indebted' to Chesterton's ballad, particularly in the similarity of Galadriel's role to that of the Virgin Mary in The Ballad of the White Horse. Clausen also saw Tolkien's Dwarves, Elves and Men, somewhat incongruously, as parallels of Chesterton's Saxons, Celts and Romans. The basic structure of the two works is similar, in Clausen's view, because both tell the story of a war between good and evil forces in which an alliance of the forces of good, despite all the odds, gains the victory against the vastly more powerful forces of evil. In both works the culmination of events is the return of the king to his rightful state. Clausen also alludes to the symbolism implicit in the fact that Gandalf's horse, Shadowfax, is the archetypal white horse of English legend.

One suspects that Clausen has read too much into the similarities between the two books, some of which are surely no more than coincidental or superficial. Although Tolkien was well acquainted with Chesterton's Ballad, admiring it greatly as a young man before becoming more critical of its undoubted flaws in later years, the extent of his scholarship suggests that his direct indebtedness to Chesterton must be limited. Yet regardless of the alleged nature of Chesterton's direct influence upon Tolkien, there is considerable evidence of his indirect influence and there are clearly discernible links of affinity between the two men.

One of the most notable of these is the sense of wonder which is an essential part of both men's work, and indeed of both men's outlook and philosophy. In *The Lord of the Rings* the enigmatic figure of Tom Bombadil seems to embody this Chestertonian sense of wonder, in which wisdom and innocence are unified, to a sublime degree: 'Tom sang most of the time, but it was chiefly nonsense, or else perhaps a strange language unknown to the hobbits, an ancient language whose words were mainly those of wonder and delight.'[24]

Tom Bombadil also appears to be Chestertonian paradox personified. Older than the world he is perennially young. He has the wisdom to wonder, the wisdom *of* wonder, which sees through worldly cynicism. He has childlike innocence without childish naïvete. These qualities are also present in the character of Quickbeam, an ent who is introduced to the hobbits by Treebeard:

> All that day they walked about in the woods with him, singing, and laughing, for Quickbeam often laughed. He laughed if the sun came out from behind a cloud, he laughed if they came upon a stream or spring: then he stooped and splashed his feet and head with water; he laughed sometimes at some sound or whisper in the trees. Whenever he saw a rowan-tree he halted a while with his arms stretched out, and sang, and swayed as he sang.[25]

T. A. Shippey, author of *The Road to Middle-earth*, referred to the infectious nature of this sense of wonder in Tolkien's work when he said that Tolkien had 'turned me into an observer. Tolkien turns people into birdwatchers, tree spotters, hedgerow-grubbers.'[26] This was certainly one of Tolkien's intentions, springing from his belief that one of the highest functions of fairy stories was the recovery of a clear view of reality:

> we need recovery. We should look at green again, and be startled anew (but not blinded) by blue and yellow and red ... This recovery fairy-stories help us to make ...

Recovery (which includes return and renewal of health) is a re-gaining – regaining of a clear view. I do not say 'seeing things as they are' and involve myself with the philosophers, though I might venture to say 'seeing things as we are (or were) meant to see them' – as things apart from ourselves. We need, in any case, to clean our windows; so that the things seen clearly may be freed from the drab blur of triteness or familiarity ...

Of course, fairy-stories are not the only means of recovery, or prophylactic against loss. Humility is enough. And there is (especially for the humble) *Mooreeffoc*, or Chestertonian Fantasy. *Mooreeffoc* is a fantastic word, but it could be seen written in every town in this land. It is Coffee-room, viewed from the inside through a glass door, as it was seen by Dickens on a dark London day, and it was used by Chesterton to denote the queerness of things that have become trite, when they are seen suddenly from a new angle.[27]

Perhaps the bonds of affinity between Tolkien and Chesterton are displayed most explicitly in their shared respect for tradition. In 1909 Chesterton had defended traditionalism by labelling it the philosophy of the Tree:

I mean that a tree goes on growing, and therefore goes on changing; but always in the fringes surrounding something unchangeable. The innermost rings of the tree are still the same as when it was a sapling; they have ceased to be seen, but they have not ceased to be central. When the tree grows a branch at the top, it does not break away from the roots at the bottom; on the contrary, it needs to hold more strongly by its roots the higher it rises with its branches. That is the true image of the vigorous and healthy progress of a man, a city, or a whole species.[28]

A keen sense of tradition was as important to Tolkien as it was to Chesterton and the whole of *The Lord of the Rings* resonates with its presence. Yet it is interesting, and perhaps not completely coincidental, that the mythological figure that Tolkien uses to embody this principle of tradition is Treebeard, a tree-like creature who was the oldest living being in the whole of Middle-earth. Treebeard appears to be Tolkien's personification of Chesterton's philosophy of the Tree.

When Pippin and Merry had first seen Treebeard they felt that the wisdom of the ages could be glimpsed in the depths of his eyes:

> Those deep eyes were now surveying them, slow and solemn, but very penetrating. They were brown, shot with a green light. Often afterwards Pippin tried to describe his first impressions of them.
>
> 'One felt as if there was an enormous well behind them, filled up with ages of memory and long, slow, steady thinking; but their surface was sparkling with the present: like sun shimmering on the outer leaves of a vast tree, or on the ripples of a very deep lake. I don't know, but it felt as if something that grew in the ground – asleep, you might say, or just feeling itself as something between root-tip and leaf-tip, between deep earth and sky had suddenly waked up, and was considering you with the same slow care that it had given to its own inside affairs for endless years.'[29]

Of course, this traditionalist imagery is rooted in the Catholicism which Chesterton and Tolkien shared, serving as a timely reminder that the bonds of affinity between them subsist within a greater well-spring of inspiration from which both men drank thirstily. Like a host of other Christian writers before and since, Tolkien was concerned principally with what the critic Lin Carter described in her study of *The Lord of the Rings* as 'the eternal verities of human nature'.[30] What was important to all the writers of the Catholic literary revival were not the accidental trappings of everyday life, the 'stuff' of soap operas, but the essential nature of everlasting life, not what human society was becoming but what humanity was being, not the peripheral but the perennial. This was the animus at the very core of the revival heralded by Newman, a revival which enshrined the belief that the highest function of art was the expression of the highest common factors of human life and not the lowest common denominators, life's loves and not its lusts. It is by these standards that Tolkien's work should be judged and it is by these standards that he shines forth as one of the *illustrissimi* of the revival of which he was part.

NOTES

1. *The Tablet*, 23 September 1989.

2. Humphrey Carpenter (ed.), *The Letters of J. R. R. Tolkien*, London: Allen & Unwin, 1981, p. 172.

3. George Sayer, interview with the author, 3 September 1997.

4. Carpenter, *The Letters of J. R. R. Tolkien*, p. 172.

5. Ibid., p. 172.

6. Ibid., p. 288.

7. Ibid.

8. Ibid.

9. George Levine, *The Boundaries of Fiction: Carlyle, Macaulay, Newman*, Princeton: Princeton University Press, 1968, p. 165.

10. John Henry Newman, *Discourses to Mixed Congregations*, pp. 283–4, quoted in William Samuel Lilly (ed.), *A Newman Anthology*, London: Dobson, 1949 edn., pp. 274–5.

11. Maisie Ward, *Gilbert Keith Chesterton*, London: Sheed and Ward, 1944, p. 551.

12. John Henry Newman, *Callista: A Tale of the Third Century*, London: Burns and Oates, 1885 edn., pp. 248–50.

13. J. R. R. Tolkien, *The Lord of the Rings*, London: Allen & Unwin, 1978, p. 1069.

14. J. R. R. Tolkien, *The Silmarillion*, London: Allen & Unwin, 1979, p. 20.

15. Ibid., p. 20.

16. Francis Thompson, *Collected Poems*, Sevenoaks, Kent: Fisher Press, 1992, p. 274.

17. Gerard Manley Hopkins, *Selected Poems*, Oxford University Press, 1991, p. 26.

18. G. K. Chesterton, *The Victorian Age in Literature*, London: Williams and Norgate, 1913, pp. 16–17.

19. *Observer*, 13 December 1925.

20. Carpenter, *The Letters of J. R. R. Tolkien*, p. 250.

21. Chesterton, *The Victorian Age in Literature*, p. 17.

22. G. K. Chesterton, *William Cobbett*, London: Hodder & Stoughton, 1925, pp. 14–15.

23. *South Atlantic Bulletin*, 39, No. 2, May 1974, pp. 10–16.

24. Tolkien, *The Lord of the Rings*, p. 162.

25. Ibid., p. 504.

26. Visual Corporation Limited, *A Film Portrait of J. R. R. Tolkien*.

27. J. R. R. Tolkien, *The Monsters and the Critics and Other Essays*, London: Allen & Unwin, 1983, p. 146.

28. *Church Socialist Quarterly*, January 1909.

29. Tolkien, *The Lord of the Rings*, pp. 484–5.

30. Lin Carter, *Tolkien: A Look Behind The Lord of the Rings*, New York: Ballantine, 1969, pp. 93–4.

10

A Far-off Gleam of the Gospel:
Salvation in Tolkien's The Lord of the Rings
Colin Gunton

Colin Gunton is Professor of Christian Doctrine in the Department of Theology and Religious Studies at King's College, London. The following article first appeared in the King's Theological Review *(Vol. 12, No. 1), in 1989.*

Some years ago, J. R. R. Tolkien's *The Lord of the Rings* was presented in dramatized form on the radio. In a preview of the production, two critics discussed what one of them called Tolkien's 'flawed masterpiece'. It was the reason given for the flaw which was of particular interest: what the great book lacks, one of them remarked, is a truly sacrificial death. There are, of course, deaths in the book, and, indeed, Gandalf goes through something like a death and resurrection in his fight with the Balrog. Whatever happens, and it seems that he does not die,[1] there is a near death and a resulting transfiguration. The interesting point, however, is not in the book, but in the fact that the critic made that remark. Why did he believe that in a heroic study of this kind there is something lacking if there is no sacrificial death? He was not, so far as I could see, speaking as a Christian. In any case, it has to be remembered that Tolkien asks that we do not attempt to see the book as a kind of Christian allegory (p. 8). Yet in some way or other, in our modern society which is supposed to have left religion behind, here was an apparently secular critic arguing for the necessity of this very religious component in a story. That is the puzzle with which I want to begin this paper.

The Lord of the Rings may not be an overtly theological book, but it is certainly in a broad sense about salvation. It is about the winning back of Middle-earth from the powers of evil. In that respect, of course, a large proportion of our art and literature is about salvation: about achieving the good life on the good earth. And in much of that art and literature three themes recur with remarkable regularity: 'salvation', or the creation of the conditions of a truly human life on earth, is understood with the help of a range of imagery coming from three main sources.

The first we have met already: it is the idea of sacrifice. Why have so many cultures had the practice of sacrifice? Why is it that in our language the word *sacrifice* continues to recur in many contexts, even though in so changed a meaning from the original? I want to suggest that it is because it appeals to something very deep in our human experience of life in the world. It has to do, at least in part, with pollution and its removal. When we have done something of which we are ashamed, we often feel dirty or unclean. And not only ourselves: we know that the world around takes on something of the pollution. The anthropologist Mary Douglas has suggested that many of our hygiene rituals are often more than merely hygienic. The rigour and fervour with which they are often performed suggests that they appeal to something deeper: to an almost religious feeling of uncleanness which must somehow or other be wiped away.[2]

As we know from some of their tragic dramas, the Greeks believed that certain evil acts brought pollution on the cities where their perpetrators lived. Oedipus' murder of his father and marriage to his widowed mother, even though done – apparently – unawares, brought to his land a pollution which could not be cleansed until his guilt was admitted and requited – by a kind of sacrifice. The fact that these plays, like those of Shakespeare, still speak so profoundly to us, suggest that we meet here something universal in the human condition. The ancient Israelites went deeper, in a realization that the sense of uncleanness derived from the disruption of their relation with their God. God is holy, and cannot bear to look on iniquity. Therefore if the worshipper is to come before him, there must be a cleansing. The sacrificial system developed partly to meet that need. It is significant that in sacrifice there must be offered to God nothing that is unclean: nothing that shares in the pollutedness it is designed to cleanse. If the worshipper is truly to come to God, uncleanness must be purged by means of a gift that is free from all taint. Sacrifice, then, is a notion that sees salvation in terms of the removal of pollution. More positively, it is about coming to our maker in the fullness of our humanity: of living before God and each other with the pure heart that cannot be achieved unless God provides the means of its cleansing.

The second way of speaking about salvation uses a range of notions taken from the law court. Here, at the centre is not uncleanness but ideas of right and wrong. Just as we sometimes feel unclean when we have erred, here we feel that we have broken the law or the moral code. In some modern circles, that would be thought to be an old-fashioned way of speaking. Are not moral codes simply conveniences, ways of ordering society, or, if the taste be Marxist, the way by which the ruling classes persuade the proletariat to remain submissive? I would like to argue for the contrary: that it is impossible to maintain a total cynicism about systems of rules and laws, because without structures of law and morality we are unable to be human. Of course, laws do become burdensome, and are sometimes used by oppressive rulers to maintain their own interest. But without some form of order, some structure, the human being cannot be free. To have the kind of absolute freedom that existentialists sometimes recommend is a recipe for both nervous and social breakdown.

Indeed, part of the problem of the modern world, with its pervasive and disastrous[3] breakdown in belief in moral objectivity, is that the attempt has been made to live as if all values are centred in ourselves. Modern thinkers who urge shapeless, empty freedom are in that respect at odds with the wisdom of the ages and the nature and needs of human community. What I have rashly called the wisdom of the ages is shown by the fact that almost all societies have believed that salvation has to do with living in harmony with the way that the universe is. It can be freely admitted that beliefs about what that is vary enormously, for that does not invalidate the main point: that the near universal experience of the human race is that the good life has something to do with living in the *right* way, and that our instinctive feelings of right and wrong are in some way related to that experience. To speak in such a way takes us some distance from direct appeal to legal metaphor and imagery, but that is because such direct appeal is not the chief concern of this paper. What is of interest in our context is the relation between conceptions of the kind of world we live in and our beliefs about right and wrong. In what sense are our human actions and choices to do with reality, and reality understood in a wide sense? We shall see that this is one of the concerns underlying Tolkien's writing.

The third set of pictures comes from the battlefield. According to this tradition, the world is a great battleground between good and evil, light and darkness, and therefore life is a battle in which we take one side or the other. Just as there have been many conceptions of the way right and wrong are written into the structure of things, there have been many expressions and understandings of the battle. Sometimes it has been held that there are two powers, of almost equal strength, who wage an eternal battle in which the human race is in some way involved. But, whatever the differences, the central concern remains the same: to see the moral life as a real struggle against evil and salvation as a kind of victory of light over darkness.

Once again, the Christian tradition has a distinctive way of expressing the matter. According to it, there is a battle, God's battle, to be fought. But because it is a battle God has won and is going to win, Christian theology has a distinctive understanding of the nature of evil. The powers of evil have, theologically, two characteristics. First, they are really evil: evil is not merely in the mind as some philosophers have suggested, but is a force which enslaves the good creation. Evil is an essentially alien power which corrupts and destroys the work of God, and so has to be destroyed. Despite this – and this is the second point – evil is not as real or as powerful as the good. It is something that exists only by feeding upon the good, like a parasite. So, according to the old traditions, devils are fallen angels: the good corrupted.

In this tradition of thought, however, evil is less real than good because it is destined to be destroyed. The outcome is that, according to the Gospel, the Christian life is a kind of battle, fought in the light of the victory that God has already won. 'Take therefore the whole armour of God ...'; 'Our fight is against principalities and powers ...' (Ephesians 6:11f). Whatever the writer means by that, we can see that he is drawing on a universal or near universal human experience of evil as a foe to be conquered. If, as sometimes happens, we feel today that money, technocracy and the weapons of war threaten to take control of civilization, we can share something of that world of thought. It is a way of understanding the plight of our world, apart from salvation and the grace of God. I believe, also, that it is from this particular world of imagery that Tolkien takes his chief cue in his great story, but that at the same time he is able to draw freely also on the two other clusters of metaphors that we have identified.

One way of understanding *The Lord of the Rings* is as a telling of a tale of the struggle against the powers of darkness that is life on earth. It is not, as we have seen, an explicitly Christian work. Yet it can be argued that it is indeed concerned with the universal human condition, as, in a different way, is the Christian faith. Is there any basis for such a claim in the work of Tolkien as a whole? That question must first be faced if such a theological treatment of Tolkien is not to appear a version of the allegorizing that he rejected. Two considerations in defence of a theological examination of *The Lord of the Rings* can be cited.

First there is evidence that Tolkien held a view that there are constant features to be found in human nature, constants that for him were reflected in the very existence and nature of language. T. A. Shippey refers to a remark of one of Tolkien's critics who was, he believes, somewhere close to the truth in 'claiming that Tolkien was really interested in the eternal verities of human nature'.[4] Despite this, Shippey points out that one must be very careful in using such terms, in view of the fact that Tolkien worked not from ideas but from words (so that any systematic theologian using his work as a means to a theological end must be exceedingly wary). Yet 'isn't there something underneath the nets of custom that remains the same?' (p. 67). Shippey believes that there is, and traces through some of Tolkien's writing what he calls a continuum of greed. Numerous characters display, in different forms, a form of this vice so that ' "the great corporate sin" (C. S. Lewis) of modernity must have had some ancient origin' (p. 68). That is to say, the shape that Tolkien's writing takes betrays at least awareness of some attempt at universality.

The second piece of evidence comes from Tolkien himself, and must again be used with caution in view of the essentially allusive way in which he speaks. In his paper 'On Fairy Stories' Tolkien speaks of the artist's calling to be the creator of a 'secondary world' which has its own truth and can at the same time throw light on the primary world in which we live. Or rather, and the choice of words is significant, the artist is not so much creator as *sub-creator*.[5] Such a distinction is essentially theological in content, for it suggests a belief that there is only one to whom we can ascribe the act of creation. The human artist can operate only at a secondary, lower, level, by divine gift. Humphrey Carpenter includes the following in his report or reconstruction of the famous conversation of 19 September 1931 between Tolkien, C. S. Lewis and Hugo Dyson. They are discussing the claim of Owen Barfield that myths, though beautiful and moving, are lies:

> *No*, said Tolkien. *They are not lies* ...
>
> Man is not ultimately a liar. He may pervert his thought into lies, but he comes from God, and it is from God that he draws his ultimate ideals ... Not merely the abstract thoughts of man *but also his imaginative inventions* must originate with God, and in consequence reflect something of eternal truth. In making a myth, in practising 'mythopoeia' and peopling the world with elves and dragons and goblins, a story-teller ... is actually fulfilling God's purpose, and reflecting a splintered fragment of the true light.[6]

Armed with such encouragement, but realizing also its limits, I shall proceed to observe *The Lord of the Rings* through the eyes given by the gospel, and suggest all kinds of interesting parallels between the two.

The first – and most obvious – point is that the book is about a titanic struggle between the powers of good and evil. On the one side are the forces of light: the free people, hobbits, those men who have not fallen into the thraldom of the Dark Lord and various other groups – groups that are often at odds with each other in the normal run of things. Over against these are the servants of Sauron, the Dark Lord, whose aim is to bring all into subjection to himself. The power of Sauron derives from the ring of power, which he forged long ago, but which has gone missing, found, apparently accidentally, by the hobbit Bilbo Baggins during an earlier quest. As the story opens, the powers of evil are regrouping, building up their strength after an earlier defeat. Their final victory depends upon the recovery of the ring: and that, as they are beginning to discover, is in the distant land of the Shire.

Frodo's quest is to destroy the power of the Dark Lord by taking the ring from the Shire and casting it down the furnace where it was forged, in the very heart of the enemy's domain. The way he goes about it is strongly marked by Christian notions. If we recall Jesus' temptation by the devil to worship him and gain power over all the cities of the world, we shall see the point of Frodo's behaviour. Again and again, actors in the drama are tempted to use the ring to overcome the Dark Lord. But Frodo, taught by Gandalf who, like him, has some of the marks of a Christ figure, realizes that to use evil, even in the battle against evil, is to become enslaved by it. The Dark Lord might be overcome, but those who overcome him will in their turn be corrupted into playing the same role. The ring enslaves those who use it, even those who lust after it, as the tragedy of Boromir demonstrates. Similarly, Gollum, the wretched creature from whom Bilbo had first stolen the ring, is totally eaten up and destroyed by its evil power. Early in the story, it becomes evident that Bilbo himself has used the ring so much that without virtually being forced to do so by Gandalf, he could not give it up. It unaccountably finds its way from the mantelpiece where it was to be left for Frodo, not yet in its power, back into Bilbo's pocket, and there is a struggle of wills before he can be persuaded to give it up (pp. 45f). Thus at the very outset we are given indications of the dread power that the ring exerts upon all who come near it.

At the other end of the story, at the crack of doom where the ring is to be cast for its destruction, we find that Frodo has so long carried the hideous article that he has joined those in thrall to the ring and cannot voluntarily give it up. It is perhaps the most brilliant and sure touch of the author that he leaves it to the even more enslaved Gollum to bite the ring from Frodo's finger, and, falling into the inferno, to find for himself the rest of death and for the world release from the evil power. Here we see two themes that awake echoes from Christian thought. First, is the fact that, although the opportunity to kill Gollum had presented itself often enough, Frodo had refused to give in to what was little more than a desire for revenge, just as Jesus had resisted his own particular temptations. Had he succumbed, the outcome could not have been the same. And second, there is the fact pointed out by my colleague, Brian Horne, that here we have a kind of doctrine of providence. Gandalf has already predicted that Gollum may have his own positive contribution to make to the outcome of the story (p. 73). The fact that when Frodo, enslaved at the last, cannot free himself of his obsession, it is the despised and wretched creature through whom release comes, is the work of a providence for whose working we have been prepared in previous stages of the story.

And there is something more to be said about the parallels between this aspect of the story and Christian theology. We noted before that evil is parasitic upon the good: it has an awful power, it corrupts and destroys, and yet has no true reality of its own. So it is with Tolkien's depiction of evil. The ring-wraiths represent some of the most horrifyingly evil agencies in literature. They are wraiths, only half real, but of a deadly and dreadful power. Their cries evoke despair – the incapacity to act – and terror in the forces of light. Their touch brings a dreadful coldness, like the coldness of Dante's hell. And yet they are finally insubstantial. When the ring is melted in the furnaces of Mount Doom, they 'crackled, withered, and went out' (p. 982). Similarly, just as the devils of Christian mythology are fallen angels, so all the creatures of the Dark Lord are hideous parodies of creatures from the true creation: goblins of elves, trolls of those splendid creatures the ents, and so on (p. 507). Evil is the corruption of good, monstrous in power yet essentially parasitic.[7]

But the most marked parallel with Christian thought is to be found at the very heart of the story. *The Lord of the Rings* can best be seen as the telling of a tale of the battle of light against darkness, good against evil, which has interesting parallels to and borrowings from Christian theology. Like Jesus, Frodo goes into the very heart of the enemy's realm in order to defeat him. And like him he is essentially weak and defenceless in worldly terms, but finally strong and invincible because he refuses to use the enemy's methods. The hobbits could almost be seen as childish or clownish figures but for the repeated references to their underlying physical and moral endurance. Their smallness and weakness become their strength, because the rulers of this age overlook them, so that the stone that was rejected becomes the head of the corner. Again and again we are reminded of biblical texts about the way the power of God works not through the great forces of history but through the cross. Too much must not be made of this, of course. But it seems to me that Tolkien's depiction of the war of good against evil has too many interesting parallels with the biblical story of Christ's victory on the cross to be ignored.

Nor should it be forgotten that there are aspects of the story that echo the two other ways of speaking of salvation also. Whatever the point made by the radio critic, there is an element of sacrifice. At the end of the story, it becomes clear that Frodo has worn himself out in the struggle, and departs, in a kind of death, across the waters from the Grey Havens. It is not a sacrificial death, but something very like it. He has worn himself out in the struggle with evil, and does not live to enjoy the new peace and contentment he has brought to the Shire. He is like Moses in seeing but not enjoying the promised land, for he is too worn to return to the old life. Similarly, if I am right in seeing a link between sacrifice and cleansing, it is to be noted that there is a chapter called 'The Scouring of the Shire'. The escaping forces of evil, represented by the wizard corrupted by greed and ambition, make their way to the Shire and pollute it, destroying nature and introducing into the Shire pointless and filthy industries. Equally significant is the fact that wherever the servants of Sauron are to be found, there is pollution and decay. The orcs wantonly destroy trees. Like the renegade wizard, Saruman (p. 494), the orcs do not care for growing things, but delight in wanton destruction. In and near the land of Mordor, all is devastation and decay: it is a very abomination of desolation. The last part of Frodo's journey into Mordor is over a dead and dreary land, virtually empty of plant life and the water that maintains it in being. Where evil conquers, there is filth, devastation and death. Frodo's great sacrifice is to have taken the weight of that foulness upon him in order to cleanse the land for the return of life.

Again, if justice in the broader sense is about living in peace with the neighbour, each under vine and fig tree, we see also a concern for righteousness in Tolkien's vision of the scoured Shire. No doubt Tolkien's vision of life in the Shire owes something to idealized pictures of rural England, but that should not detract from the chief point. The hobbits are an idealized – and sometimes rather sentimentalized? – version of the meek who shall inherit the earth. They are not interested in world domination, or economic and technological development for its own sake. The great battle was fought to enable hobbits and men to live in peace in their homes; it was to provide the conditions for the development of community.[8] Perhaps it is here that we can discern another central Christian influence on Tolkien's writing. At the heart of the Christian gospel is the concern with persons. To be human is to be a person in relation with other persons, a way of being that is possible only when the relationship is restored by the sacrificial death of Christ on the cross and the triumph crowned by his resurrection from the dead.

Tolkien's strength here is to have seen something of the importance of the person. To fall into the power of the evil one is to be depersonalized. Nowhere is this better illustrated than by the portrait of the herald of Sauron who rides to meet the army of Gondor as it waits apparently foolhardily at the gates of Mordor. 'The Lieutenant of the Tower of Baradur he was, and his name is remembered in no tale; for he himself had forgotten it, and he said: "I am the mouth of Sauron."' (p. 922). To serve the power of evil is to lose one's name, that which we gain by virtue of our loving relationship with others; it is to enter a slavery in which our very identity is taken away. Similarly, wherever the Dark Lord's influence is felt, human relations are in danger. His power is to be found even among his foes, where it causes friends to fall out and quarrel (p. 366), but, more notably, in the fact that his own servants fight each other savagely. Evil alienates and destroys. It is against the depersonalizing of Middle-earth with its accompanying slavery, pollution and lawlessness that the titanic battle takes place.

There are, of course, elements of magic and militarism in the tale which prevent us from taking it with too literal an allegorizing. But underlying the whole is a sure sense that evil is a continuing threat which has to be fought. Frodo's achievement, like Christ's, is eschatological but not the eschaton. The possibility of a return to slavery remains, as the words of Gandalf make clear:

> Other evils there are that may come; for Sauron himself is but a servant or emissary. Yet it is not our part to master all the tides of the world, but to do what is in us for the succour of those years wherein we are set, uprooting the evil in the fields that we know, so that those who live after may have clean earth to till. What weather they shall have is not ours to rule. (p. 913)

Those words of Gandalf are like the allusions we have discerned in *The Lord of the Rings* to the action of providence: they take us near, but not quite, to theology proper. The stopping short is as it should be, for, as we have seen, Tolkien does not write as a theologian but as the teller of a story. In that telling he shares the directedness of so much art and literature to the theme of salvation, understood in its broadest sense. Outlined above was his use not only of the great theme of the battle of light against darkness, but also of other images of salvation. It was also shown that other echoes of Christian theology were to be discerned: the ways in which Frodo's bearing and behaviour echo that of Christ, and the overall concern for the reconciliation of persons in the context of a redeemed earth. What are the main differences that are to be seen?

The first is considerable. In the opening chapter of Ephesians, there is set before us a vision of salvation, which, the author makes clear, is not simply some religious idea but the completion of the creator's work for the whole creation: 'a purpose ... to unite all things in (Christ), things in heaven and things on earth' (Ephesians 1:9f). There we see immediately a radical difference from Tolkien's tale. The latter does sometimes reveal a nostalgic pessimism: the old order has gone, is tired and soiled, and will never return. Elves will disappear, and the richness of Middle-earth diminish. It is a rather backward looking vision: the best was in the past, and will not return. By contrast, the vision of Ephesians is eschatological, and reminds us that hope is a primary Christian virtue. The creation looks forward to an end. It has, indeed, been subjected to futility, so that it groans like a woman in childbirth, but the work of Christ is at once to restore and to perfect.

The second major difference is that in the Christian version of the three great themes they are transfigured, take new and radically different shape by being understood through the lens provided by the life and death of Jesus. The crucial point here is that for Christian soteriology that life and death are not simply the victory of a man against temptation, the sacrificial death of a man on behalf of others and the death of the just who dies for the unjust. They are indeed all of these things. But they are also much more. As all of those things they are the act and involvement of God in and for our world. The victory over evil gains its universal significance by virtue of the fact that it is the power of God exercised through the weakness and suffering of a man. The sacrifice that is the cleansing of the earth is God's giving up to death of his Son, the one through whom the world was made, so that the creation may also through him be brought to its completion. The death of the just for the unjust is undergone in order that relationships we destroy by our injustice may be forgiven and rebuilt. What Tolkien helps us to see, by both illumination and contrast, is that in the light of the cross of the Lord all the three themes are transfigured.

In both illumination and contrast it is noteworthy that the diagnosis of the ill is very similar: fearful and demonic evil, and the whole creation in thrall to desolating pollution and war. Tolkien's story can accordingly be seen as a vivid portrayal of the universal effects of human sin, countered with a mythological and highly illuminating account of their overcoming. What is different in the Christian scheme is the twofold emphasis: that such evil can be defeated and cleansed only by God, and that it can be done also only by a truly representative child of Adam. At the heart of the matter is the incarnation. The cleansing and completion of the creation comes about when the eternal Word of God, through whom all things were made, took flesh so that he might himself, as true man, bring together God and the world which evil had sundered. Interestingly enough, there is even a kind of parallel to this in Tolkien's myth. 'What was Gandalf? In what far time and place did he come into the world, and when would he leave it?' (p. 787: echoes of some of the language Jesus uses of himself in John's Gospel).

What the Christian gospel offers, by contrast, is not myth, but incarnation. God comes not to fight some mythological battle, but to engage as man in the heart of the human struggle for righteousness. And it is around that man that a community is formed, as his body, to realize the salvation that he won. That is why the Christian faith is concrete in a different way from *The Lord of the Rings*. The latter gains its strength, as we have seen, in part from its embodying in a story of universal appeal features which both answer to and illuminate the world in which we live. It is myth in the best sense of the word, encapsulating in concrete narrative central ways in which the human quest for salvation comes to expression. The former is concrete in that it embodies in a lived form not so much a quest for salvation as the recapitulation of human life in the victory, sacrifice and justification which is the life, death and resurrection of the incarnate Word.

The conclusion of this paper is, therefore, that the two focuses of its argument, Tolkien's masterpiece and the Christian tradition of atonement theology, can be mutually illuminating. Both are allowed to be what they separately are: a great story and a theology of salvation. Yet the story without doubt borrows from the Christian tradition in which its writer stood, while the theology cannot be expressed except in the metaphors which the literature of humanity provides. A final point brings the two even closer together, and provides something of a justification from Tolkien himself of the rash enterprise here attempted. At the close of 'On Fairy Stories' Tolkien reflects on the distinctive 'joy' that is the outcome of successful fantasy. It can be, he says, 'a far-off gleam or echo of *evangelium* in the real world', so that it may even enable us better to understand the true gospel:

The birth of Christ is the eucatastrophe of the story of the Incarnation. This story begins and ends in joy. It has pre-eminently the 'inner consistency of reality'. There is no tale ever told that men would rather find was true, and none which so many sceptical men have accepted as true on its own merits. For the Art of it has the supremely convincing tone of Primary Art, that is, of Creation.[9]

May not, then, one reason for taking Tolkien's splendid tale seriously theologically be that it is in so many respects 'a far-off gleam or echo of *evangelium*'; perhaps, indeed, not so very far-off a gleam?[10]

NOTES

1. J. R. R. Tolkien, *The Lord of the Rings*, single volume edn., London: Allen & Unwin, 1968, pp. 523f. Whether he dies is not clearly stated in his narrative of the struggle, though compare p. 536: 'I have not passed through fire and death to bandy crooked words ...' and p. 607: 'I am Gandalf the White, who has returned from death.' Further references to the work will be in parentheses in the text.

2. Mary Douglas, *Purity and Danger: An Analysis of the Concepts of Pollution and Taboo*, London: Ark Paperbacks, 1984 (first edn., 1966), pp. 29–40.

3. See especially Alasdair MacIntyre, *After Virtue*, London: Duckworth, 1981, and *Whose Justice? Which Rationality?*, London: Duckworth, 1988; and Allan Bloom, *The Closing of the American Mind*, London: Penguin, 1988.

4. T. A. Shippey, *The Road to Middle-earth*, London: Allen & Unwin, 1982, p. 19.

5. J. R. R. Tolkien, 'On Fairy Stories', in *Tree and Leaf*, London: Allen & Unwin, 1964, pp. 11–70 (pp. 43–50).

6. Humphrey Carpenter, *The Inklings: C. S. Lewis, J. R. R. Tolkien and their Friends*, London: Allen & Unwin, 1978, p. 43. See also *The Letters of J. R. R. Tolkien*, ed. H. Carpenter, London: Allen & Unwin, 1981, p. 144: 'Myth and fairy story must, as all art, reflect and contain in solution elements of moral and religious truth (or error), but not explicit, not in the known form of the primary "real" world.'

7. It will be seen from these remarks that I find somewhat more consistent a theology of evil in *The Lord of the Rings* than does Shippey, who seems to me to make the mistake of drawing too absolute a distinction between 'inner' and 'objective' evil, op. cit. pp. 107–11.

8. 'C. Williams who is reading it all says the great thing is that its *centre* is not in strife and war and heroism (though they are understood and depicted) but in freedom, peace and ordinary life and good living. Yet he agrees that these very things require the existence of a great world outside the Shire – lest they should grow stale by custom and turn into the humdrum ...' Tolkien, *Letters* pp. 105f.

9. 'On Fairy Stories', op. cit., pp. 62f.

10. I am grateful to Francis Watson for criticism of a first draft of this paper, as a result of which it is, I believe, much better than it would otherwise have been.

11

ROOT AND TREE: THE GROWTH OF
TOLKIEN'S WRITINGS
RICHARD JEFFERY

Richard Jeffery, a copy editor living near Oxford, met Tolkien in 1956. During their meeting Tolkien spoke 'with immense enthusiasm' about two of the myths from the still unpublished Silmarillion. *This essay is a shortened and adapted version of a talk which Mr Jeffery gave to the Oxford C. S. Lewis Society in February 1994.*

Reactions to *The Lord of the Rings* and the related books range from something like 'great works which repay any amount of attention' through 'entertaining and interesting in parts' to 'shapeless and childish, wasting the readers' time and corrupting their judgement'. C. S. Lewis's reactions, to *The Lord of the Rings*, *The Hobbit*, and a version of a part of *The Silmarillion*, were close to the upper end of this range. I think he was quite right, but some of the criticisms do hold for some parts of the work, without, I believe, undermining the whole.

Tolkien's importance as an imaginative writer rests with these three interlinked books, *The Hobbit*, *The Lord of the Rings*, *The Silmarillion* (I would include the little book of verses *The Adventures of Tom Bombadil*, which is introduced as a collection of verses written by Hobbits of the Shire, making it a kind of appendix to Book One of *The Lord of the Rings*). His independent short imaginative works, and his essays on stories and language, are interesting and some of them are attractive, but not important in their own right –

the essays might be important, but their conclusions are not very clear, so that they take effect mainly by helping to cast light on the main fiction. His professional work on Old and Middle English is powerful and influential, but its quantity is very limited.

The interlinked books make up a unique and outstanding life's work, not as a single coherent imaged world and history, which they are not entirely, but as three books of very different kinds, with very different strengths, making an extraordinarily comprehensive whole partly by adding to each other, partly by defects in one contrasting with qualities in another. Their interconnections are very complex because in each case Tolkien drew on what he had previously written not only as a direct source for some of the characters and background, but as the main indirect source for types of story and details of episodes – this is very much more central to the character of *The Hobbit* and *The Lord of the Rings* than any parallels with other people's works. I want to go through some of the history of how the three books grew, because I think it helps in understanding their natures.

Christopher Tolkien remarks that his father 'undoubtedly preserved a very high proportion of everything he ever wrote'. Not, I am sure, to preserve it for posterity, but as a kind of private stockpot or seedbed – an element altered or abandoned in its original setting might still be used in another (though in practice he far more often drew on the latest or final versions of things, published or unpublished, to re-use). Tolkien had a respect and even awe for human creative capacities, and hence for his own, which if directed slightly differently might have been arrogant and absurd, but in practice he was a perfectionist who nearly always looked forward to more perfect versions still unachieved, of fiction or non-fiction, who wanted to improve a thing further rather than publish it as it was. He worked at *The Silmarillion* on and off between the ages of twenty-four and eighty-one. Most of the elements of the story are there in *The Lost Tales* written by the time he was twenty-seven, nearly all the story is in the twenty-page summary written when he was thirty-four; this was later enlarged detail by detail in successive stages. I don't think there's any question that the form as well as the content of the published *Silmarillion* are Tolkien's work, realized by Christopher, and it is this (not the whole mass of drafts) which I call one of the three interlinked books.

The history of *The Silmarillion* is quite unusual, in that the substance of the story was fixed and written down in his youth and remained in his mind throughout his life, but he only developed the makings of a satisfactory embodiment of it after he had finished all his other major works.

How did he come to write such a thing? And why did he take it so seriously that he gradually modified what had originally come out as a number of odd and sometimes grotesque fantasies together with two curious invented vocabularies, into something powerfully enduring? Humphrey Carpenter in his biography traces the impulse to the group of young men who formed themselves into a society in Tolkien's last term at school when he was nineteen. Four of them, Tolkien, Wiseman, Gilson and Smith, stayed in fairly close touch and to some extent regarded themselves as a unity until 1916, when they were all serving in the Army or Navy and two of the four were killed. Carpenter emphasizes phrases in a letter from Smith not long before he was killed, that if he died there would still be a survivor 'to voice what I dreamed and what we all agreed on', and 'may you say the things I have tried to say long after I am not there to say them'.

But I don't believe Tolkien thought like this. He regarded creativity as altogether individual: a writer should stick to his own private individual mythology, his own blend drawn from the universal common stock. The creator of an invented language (Tolkien's two Elvish languages and his mythology were integral parts of each other from the beginning) should try to realize what a character in one story calls his own 'native language', to find the forms which specially appeal to him. I am sure that he thought of this society of four young men as giving each other inspiration and encouragement, rather than as combining to say something that they all agreed on. A few months before, he wrote to Smith after Gilson had been killed, referring to their conviction that the group of them 'had been granted some spark of fire – certainly as a body if not singly – that was destined to kindle a light, or what is the same thing, rekindle an old light in the world ... to testify for God and Truth in a more direct way even than by laying down its several lives in this war'. But this 'greatness which we three certainly meant' would have to be achieved individually: 'the greatness I meant was that of a great instrument in God's hands – a mover, a doer, even an achiever of great things, a beginner at the least of very large things'. If any of them were killed, it must be that they 'were not meant to be great – at least directly', with this kind of greatness, but with the completely different greatness of heroic self-sacrifice, inspiration and example. He continues that he still pins his hopes to 'the inspiration which we do know we all get and get from one another', and that the last time the four of them met, nearly two years before, 'was as you know followed in my own case with my finding a voice for all kinds of pent up things and a tremendous opening up of everything for me'.

When he wrote this, August 1916, he seems not to have written any of the stories of his mythology, and in the same letter he says he now has 'intense feelings more than ideas'. He had written a number of poems which contain germs of the mythology, and probably already a vocabulary of one of his Elvish languages, which means an attempt to produce words each with a sound that he felt was fitted for its meaning, and which all combined consistently into a convincing language, together with an imagination of an

Elvish people who had developed such a language, whose first response on meeting and experiencing something new would be to devise the most appropriate name for it. (Much later he put into *The Silmarillion* that the Noldorin Elves 'were changeful in speech, for they had great love of words and sought ever to find names more fit for all things that they knew or imagined'.) The earliest poems are on the lone mariner Earendel sailing to the strange lands of the furthest west and on into the sky as the Evening and Morning Star; and here the story came from the name, an Old English name Earendel, apparently meaning the Morning Star, a name with a good Germanic pedigree but which Tolkien felt to have an extraordinary beauty, different from the rougher beauty of most of Old English, so that he imagined it as somehow an echo of a much more ancient language, e-a-ren-del, and wove it into the language he was developing.

But the germ of the actual stories is not feelings about language or about sky and stars, but about the town where Edith Bratt was living. Tolkien and Edith met when he and his brother and she were lodging in the same house in Birmingham, when he was sixteen and she was nineteen (Tolkien's father had died when Tolkien was four, his mother when he was twelve; Edith was an orphan too). The summer of the following year, as Humphrey Carpenter puts it, they 'decided they were in love'. Tolkien's guardian discovered this and forbade it, and soon after his eighteenth birthday forbade them to communicate until he was twenty-one. So he waited for her from afar for three years (he seems to have assumed she was being kept in cold storage for him – she, not surprisingly, didn't feel so certain about him), wrote to her promptly on his twenty-first birthday, and for three more years they were engaged at a distance, while she was living in Warwick. They married in the spring of 1916, he was sent to France in the summer, returned with trench fever in the autumn, and began writing stories about the same time.

He used to visit his betrothed in Warwick, a city smaller and perhaps older than Oxford, far smaller and far older than Birmingham (the two towns he knew well), with an ancient castle on a hill, and many elms and other trees in and around. Near the end of the three years he wrote verses picturing it as the fading relic of the town of Kortirion built by the fairies. The enchantment spreading out from Edith and Warwick, surrounding Warwickshire was Alalminore, the Land of Elms, and the whole of Britain 'the fading isle / Where linger yet the lonely companies', 'the holy fairies and immortal elves', with Kortirion as its centre (Warwick is indeed somewhere near the centre of England and Wales, as well as of Warwickshire): 'Remember what is gone – / The magic sun that lit Kortirion!'

For a while in his mythology Britain was actually the island of the elves, moved bodily across the ocean from the far west in the course of the Faring Forth, the disastrous attempt to rescue the elves wandering in exile in the Great Lands of the world, which if it had been successful would have restored the primeval light of the Magic Sun. But this myth was never clearly formulated and was abandoned. Only the character of the Faring Forth survived in the story of a concerted campaign of elves and men against the Enemy, starting with triumphant hope and turning to the disaster of the Battle of Unnumbered Tears, which is a central episode in the long siege and war latterly turning to a series of progressive disasters and ruins which is the main story of *The Silmarillion*. The Magic Sun and Moon became the Two Trees made by the gods or archangels, as part of the creation in which the One God had allowed them to share in both designing and making: Two Trees which illuminated the world and which were destroyed by the fallen archangel, so that their light survived only where the elf-prince Fëanor had caught it in three jewels, the Silmarils. The Enemy stole these also, and Fëanor defied the gods and fought with other elves in order to pursue and make war on him. This war lasts five hundred years, quite a short time to elves but many generations to the men who become involved in it. Set in the catastrophic story of the latter part of the war are two long legends about men, the romantic epic of Beren and the elf-princess, and the tragic epic of Turin and his sister. It's fairly well known that parts of these are obviously borrowed by Tolkien: Beren from the Welsh tale of Kilhwch and Olwen from what's now called the *Mabinogion*, Turin from the Finnish *Kalevala*.

When *The Silmarillion* was published in 1977, on my first reading I was disgusted – the rumour had been that it was a complete mythology, and I had expected something like Greek or Norse mythology, with scores of interrelated stories: then practically speaking there were only two, and they weren't even original! But I believe the various echoes of existing stories (anything from Troy to the Babes in the Wood) are basic to the character of the book. It presents itself as *the* story, the original, central, fundamental story, the basic stock of the Cauldron of Story (the image that Tolkien uses in his essay 'On Fairy Stories'), of which even fragments once heard could never totally be forgotten: so that all tragic epic stories are boiled down from the story of Turin, all romances from the tale of Beren and Lúthien, while stories about gods are corruptions and distortions of the history of the archangelic Valar. I think Tolkien must have at least half-consciously thought of it like this, for he retouched and reworded his versions so many times without altering their outlines, that he must have been extremely familiar with them and aware of any parallels with anything else he knew.

So when he wrote other stories himself, *The Silmarillion* was at the back of his mind as the ultimate source of all stories. Of course it's only within its own fiction that it is this: but it is much more effective and credible in the role than the various ideas that have been seriously proposed as the source of all mythologies, because it is a story itself, complicated but sufficiently a unity – rather as in classical music a balanced symphony has a beginning, an end, and just two contrasting separate complete movements in the middle – a story which grew by contemplating existing myths as stories, not as sources of concealed meanings.

The Hobbit developed as a serial story to entertain his children; it developed out of the opening sentence 'In a hole in the ground there lived a hobbit', which he claimed came to him suddenly out of nowhere. I guess it came from a half-feeling that *hole* ought to alliterate with *rabbit*. But plainly to him it was not a cosy image of furry creatures to be indulgently contemplated; he felt *himself* to be living in a fairly safe, comfortable bourgeois hole, among his family in Oxford in the late twenties. The message to his children is first and foremost 'There are things that one should risk one's comfort and safety to go out and see and do.' (In the essay 'On Fairy Stories' he wrote, 'The dweller in the quiet and fertile plains may hear of the tormented hills and the unharvested sea and long for them in his heart. For the heart is hard though the body be soft.')

So he brings in a wizard to bounce the hobbit into an adventure, and thirteen dwarves out of Old Norse mythology to make the adventure. What adventure? In *The Silmarillion* there is just one episode where an ordinary mortal and a group of other beings go together on a quest; the one from the *Mabinogion* where an elf-king and his ten faithful followers join Beren, which is a tragic episode in which the elves are all killed, and nearly all eaten, by werewolves (at this point Beren is rescued by Lúthien herself), but Tolkien's actual source for it in Kilhwch and Olwen is not tragic, though it's fairly ruthless. *The Hobbit* inherits a realistic ruthlessness, which *The Lord of the Rings* tends to evade. Beren's companions were eaten while he and the king waited to be eaten too. Bilbo and his companions have to wait expecting to be eaten by trolls, probably by goblins, by Gollum, by wolves, by spiders, by the dragon, and Bilbo imagines they'll be eaten by bears and eagles, so that they're very much in the position of small animals with many creatures above them in the food chain: but this has developed out of a myth about human beings. In the final battle the dwarf-king Thorin is killed, and so are his young nephews, who 'died defending him with shield and body, for he was their mother's elder brother'.

Two scenes in *The Hobbit* seem to me unconvincing, both of them traditional-type stories which belong in settings where convincing details of behaviour are less relevant than here: Gandalf keeping the trolls arguing how to cook dwarves till the dawn comes and turns them to stone; and Gandalf making the dwarves appear in a long series two at a time while he tells their story to Beorn. Otherwise I find it convincing and extremely vivid, and most beautifully constructed. Up to the great mountains each episode provides something which will be needed later, the map and key, the enchanted swords, the way to read the map, Gollum's ring. After that, in successive episodes we meet and leave or escape from the wolves, the goblins, the eagles, Beorn, the elves of Mirkwood, and the men of Laketown, apparently with no consequences except that Bilbo becomes more self-reliant. But then, after the scenes with the dragon and his death, all of these reappear at the Mountain, and so does Gandalf, all quite naturally in reaction to the treasure left undefended. The consequent battle ends up the story, but it wouldn't end the desire for more episodes (in those who like this sort of thing) if it wasn't for the mortal wound and deathbed scene of Thorin, the most central character after Bilbo, reinforced by the deaths of his young and sympathetic nephews. This brings our emotional responses to a stop, so that the book can draw quietly to a close back where it started, with a few extra hobbit curlicues. *The Lord of the Rings* I find has an unconvincing climax simply because, in a story full of battles and deaths, no one who is sufficiently central or regrettable dies – repeatedly such characters are believed to be dead but turn out not to be (Frodo more than once, Gandalf, Éowyn, Faramir, Pippin). Only at the very end, with the departure of the bearers of the One Ring and the Three Rings beyond this world, is this defeat remedied.

The Silmarillion in its final form, and largely in the over-short form it had when *The Hobbit* was written, is self-contained and consistent, polished very thoroughly into what he wanted to write, quite confident (even if vague) about its audience. It might be called pure, in the sense of being of the same kind all through, but distant or withdrawn, or perhaps abstract. *The Hobbit* is likewise consistent in itself, both confident and clear about its original audience (his children); pure in the same sense, and not at all withdrawn (putting, as it were, a reader-friendly hobbit into that world), but with limitations of subject and size.

The Lord of the Rings is different: not pure and consistent but very mixed; on a very large scale in nearly every sense, but in some ways ignoring its limitations. It started in response to the publishers' request for a sequel after the encouraging reception of *The Hobbit*, and so is the only work of fiction that Tolkien wrote because he was asked to write it. The result of this, on a perfectionist who had created a whole mythology that hardly anyone had seen and two whole languages that no one at all had seen, and was torn between believing them to be of immense value and of no real value, was a huge book, which kept expanding as more episodes intruded themselves before the planned climax, as he wrote it in fits and starts over eleven years. It is rightly thought of as his central work, into which he put more of himself than into anything else, but is extremely uneven in value, increasingly so as it continues and is uncertain as to its audience.

Of the six 'books' in the three volumes of *The Lord of the Rings*, Book One was repeatedly revised and rewritten over several years; all the rest went almost straight from preliminary sketches to the final form of the story and, except for details, the final form of the text. And to my mind Book One, Frodo's journey as far as Rivendell with the other three hobbits and then with Strider, is the heart of the book; it is the only part which is practically as good as Tolkien the perfectionist could get it (some critics have included passages from it when denouncing Tolkien's style, but I think their detailed objections can be shown to be misconceived). Some people find the hobbit part irritating, but the whole has a unique compound of the qualities of a fairy-story and a myth, which gives an extraordinary power, and a sense of the strangeness and importance of the world, of familiar things, of ordinary decisions; a sense that our lives correspond deeply to this 'world being after all full of strange creatures beyond count', where a journey in any direction is likely to lead across huge tracts of empty wilderness to some quite unprecedented form of danger, or kindness, or beauty; where all those living apparently safe in their comfortable holes 'were, in fact, sheltered, though they had ceased to remember it', and might easily lose that protection: where everything depends on roots going back to remote antiquity; where also we have to carry the ring of power which brings into all ordinary decisions and relationships the temptation to try to control other people's minds – something which throws into relief that as it is they are not under our control, that they are as much independent centres of their own world of awareness as we are. Strangeness and familiarity appear beside each other in the story in a way that discloses what they mean to us in life. To me it's this book which casts a spell over all the rest of *The Lord of the Rings* and keeps the whole complexity alive. Much of the next volume and a half is almost as compelling (more in the character of myth and history, with less of the immediacy of fairy-story): Moria, Lothlórien, the Great River, the breaking of the Fellowship, Rohan, Fangorn, Gollum, the Dead Marshes and the desolation before Mordor.

It's the third volume which to my mind is a mixture of compelling parts and parts he'd have done better to rethink completely. In Gondor, all the scenes with the arrogant old ruler and with Faramir his son are remarkable, but the ordinariness of all the other people of Gondor comes out as merely flat (whereas the Rohirrim, and Aragorn, are still vivid). Gandalf, on his great horse Shadowfax, having rushed to Gondor, has far too little to do there. The three chapters with Frodo and Sam in Mordor, which surely ought to be a culmination of the earlier great scenes of awesome evil and desolation, are just dull, the orcs sound far too much like ordinary grumbling soldiers – only with Gollum's two speeches just before and at the climax does the book suddenly revert from flat to sublime. The scene where Frodo and Sam are acclaimed after their rescue and recovery is mostly only embarrassing. Most of the chapter on the Scouring of the Shire, when the hobbits of the Shire are roused to throw out the intruding Men who have taken over, is done in an objectionable way. And, as I have said, until the very end everything works out too easily, nobody whose death would be seriously distressing turns out to be really dead, Tolkien is too much inclined to pull his punches (perhaps because he was never quite clear what audience he was writing for): horrors are too much excluded from this story of a terrible war.

The Lord of the Rings starts from the material of *The Hobbit*, from Bilbo and Gandalf, the question who was Gollum and what was the Ring, and the question what was there around Bilbo's home and between there and Rivendell (the answer to this last question comes out so different from the original that the adjustments to that part of the third edition of *The Hobbit* to cover the discrepancy – changing a journey through gradually less civilized but inhabited regions up to the Edge of the World, to one through empty wilderness – only make it inconsistent with itself). At first it seems again to be following Bilbo's own story, but as Bilbo slips away from Bag End garden on a second journey, 'He jumped over a low place in the hedge at the bottom, and took to the meadows, passing into the night like a rustle of wind in the grass,' we find that we're left behind with Gandalf and Frodo. After Gandalf, seventeen years and two chapters later, also goes off and fails to return, Frodo has to leave likewise, and slips away from the garden, with his friend Pippin: 'They jumped over the low place in the hedge at the bottom and took to the fields, passing into the darkness like a rustle in the grasses.' (These two parallel passages are both derived from the same one in an early draft.) This time we find we've gone with Frodo, and the viewpoint remains almost entirely with him for the rest of Book One. The effect is very strongly that this time we actually are starting out on the journey, and that we're really sharing Frodo's view, but that it's not inevitable and might be taken away from us. In fact in the rest of the book it largely is taken from us, giving more scope but leaving us sometimes less involved. At the end of Book One the effects of his wound make his viewpoint increasingly blurred; in Book Two he wakes up in Rivendell, well again, after a long time lapse – something seems to have altered, and it seems natural that the viewpoint shifts for a moment to Gandalf, looking at the sleeping Frodo, thinking that he may turn out to be changed in an unpredictable way. Here Rivendell, its ruler Elrond, elves, and dwarves are all material directly from *The Hobbit*, but they don't fully recapture the vividness they had there: the elf and dwarf who join the fellowship and remain with us for the rest of the book don't give us the matter-of-fact sense of otherness that elves and dwarves give in *The Hobbit*. Elrond is impressive: 'Venerable he seemed as a king crowned with many winters, and yet hale as a tried warrior in the fullness of his strength. He was the Lord of Rivendell and mighty among both elves and men,' but not with the enchantment of the extraordinary description in *The Hobbit*: 'He was as noble and as fair in face as an elf-lord, as strong as a warrior, as wise as a wizard, as venerable as a king of dwarves, and as kind as summer ... Evil things did not come into that valley.'

The next few chapters re-use a lot of elements from *The Hobbit*, as vividly as in the original. This part ends by the tomb of one of Bilbo's old companions who had tried to reclaim the old dwarf-kingdom, just as *The Hobbit* ends at the deathbed of Thorin, and with a similar sense of finality. It seems very natural that Tolkien stopped at this point, uncertain how to continue: as he wrote in the second edition Foreword, 'There I halted a long while.' When he took up the story almost a year later it began to spring from different sources, from *The Silmarillion*. The travellers find parts of an old manuscript, about the attempt to refound the kingdom here nearly twenty years before, and about its destruction: '*We cannot get out. We cannot get out. They have taken the Bridge and second hall ... Drums, drums in the deep.*' I wonder what that means. The last thing written is in a trailing scrawl of elf-letters: '*they are coming.* There is nothing more' – and suddenly this story comes alive around them: a drum beating, followed by horns and sounds of goblins shouting and running; '"They are coming," cried Legolas. "We cannot get out," said Gimli.' Likewise soon elements of *The Silmarillion*, first written nearly thirty years before (or, within the story, having taken place thousands of years before), reappear: first a Balrog, a fire-demon, as in the fall of Gondolin and the rest of the ruinous wars with Morgoth – so formidable that Gandalf falls into the abyss with it. Before we've quite recovered from this we're confronted by the lady Galadriel, the last survivor of the cousins, princes of the Noldorin Elves, who defied the gods and exiled themselves to Middle-earth to regain the Silmarils. (Elrond appears in *The Silmarillion* but only as a young child – actually *The Silmarillion* had to be rearranged just a little to make a place for Galadriel, who hadn't originally been thought of.) And *The Silmarillion* continues to be a source for the rest of *The Lord of the Rings*, noticeably with the Breaking of the Fellowship at the end of this book, which is full of echoes of the story of Turin; with Denethor; with the she-monster-spider; with Sam rescuing Frodo from the tower; and with the entire geography east of the Misty Mountains, which becomes a not very complex rearrangement of *The Silmarillion* map, bringing with it the elves of Lothlórien, the ents (again, a new creation but fitted retrospectively into the fringes of the old story), the horsemen of Rohan, the ancient battles that left the desolation before Mordor.

I haven't tried much to say what these intertwined stories are about, what they're for. To those who like them they are images of the world, of mortal life, the actuality and the mystery of what there is, and of duty, loyalty and love, seen with a great deal of wisdom, and, taken together, very comprehensive. With all its defects it is *The Lord of the Rings* which to most readers is Tolkien's great, essential work, and rightly so: and with all its defects, there is no getting round it, it is one of the great essential works of imaginative fiction.

12

J. R. R. Tolkien: Master of Middle-earth
Stephen R. Lawhead

As well as being a best-selling author in the fantasy genre, writing many successful books for both adults and children, Stephen R. Lawhead has written non-fiction books and has co-authored several works with his wife, Alice Slaikeu Lawhead. The fifth and final part of his Pendragon Cycle, *entitled* Grail, *was published in September 1997. This essay was originally published in* Reality and the Vision, *edited by Philip Yancey (Word Publishing, Dallas, USA, 1990).*

I discovered J. R. R. Tolkien in exactly the same way as millions of other admirers: through the pages of *The Lord of the Rings*. I was a college student at the time, teaching an eighth-grade art class, when I noticed one of my students – a shy, overweight kid with an intellectual bent – coming to school early to pore over these thick paperbacks.

At the time, I was only dimly aware of this fantasy trilogy or its author, but they had already won legions of devoted fans around the world. Certainly, the devotion that boy lavished on those books bordered on the fanatical. Every spare moment he laboured over reams of the most intricate and exotic script: runes, he told me. Or he practised one of the elven languages he'd learned from the books – he was so enthralled with the story he even taught himself to speak elf!

'You should read these books, Mr Lawhead,' he'd say when he came to show me his latest runic epistle. 'J. R. R. Tolkien is the greatest author who ever lived.'

To be honest, his endorsement steered me away from the books for a good long time. I am contrary that way. Let anyone praise a thing too highly and I make tracks in the opposite direction.

It wasn't until seminary a few years later that I picked up a copy of *The Fellowship of the Ring*. Probably I was supposed to be reading homiletics or hermeneutics or something of similar weight, but boredom and curiosity finally got the better of me. In fact, my head was so full of the massive profundity of seminary study that ol' J. R. R. came across as a gulp of fresh air to a man drowning in mud.

His tale of hobbits and magic rings and a world inhabited by orcs, elves, dwarves, wizards, and dragons proved a perfect antidote to the arid drear of Old Testament hagiography. Within the pages of his remarkable book real 'people' lived and struggled and died. An entire universe of them!

The Tolkien Trilogy quickly became my bedtime reading, doled out in carefully measured nightly doses. I savoured each and every syllable of that shining prose.

I have always been an avid reader – some of my best friends are books. But until I cracked the cover of Professor Tolkien's classic, I had never encountered a book of such splendid magnitude, such grace, such scope and wholeness of vision. And all of it was seamless, unforced, genuine, and extremely entertaining.

Well, it made an impact. Although I was never moved to communicate in runes or begin babbling in High Elf, I learned a lasting lesson about the nature of storytelling. Through the long, elegant movements of *The Lord of the Rings* I grasped the structure of the epic, and something of the interplay of story elements, and the force of narrative.

More, I began to understand the enormous power of fiction to speak to the heart and soul of the reader, to lift the spirit, to ennoble and challenge and inspire.

These things I learned, and the learning went deep, I think. At least, it went underground for a season. For the next years saw me at *Campus Life* magazine, mastering what I could of the writing craft. I rarely thought about Tolkien's books during that time, nor did I think seriously about fiction; and hobbits hardly ever entered my conversation. But the seed Tolkien's books had sown was germinating. There in the moist, fertile darkness of my subconscious (or wherever these things sprout), the first notions of writing the sort of books I loved reading began to take root.

About this same time, I discovered the Inklings – quite by accident, as it happens. While researching an article about Tolkien for *Campus Life*, I picked up a copy of Humphrey Carpenter's biography of the professor. The author described the importance in Tolkien's life of his literary friends, a fairly informal group of Oxford academics of one sort or another who went by the name of the Inklings.

Having enjoyed Tolkien's books, I tracked down and read some of the work of some of the other Inklings – C. S. Lewis and Charles Williams especially. I enjoyed the books, but in the end it wasn't the Inklings' work that moved me. It was the informing spirit of their work, a spirit which I began to sense they all shared.

What was this peculiar spirit? I was content to wonder about this in my own slow way, gathering bits and pieces of it whenever and wherever they popped up, salting them away in my private cache.

Then one day, a few years later, I sat down at the typewriter to write a book. I was, for the first time in my life, completely free to write whatever I liked. (That is to say, I was unemployed.)

It was the worst possible time to undertake such a venture from any practical point of view. No job, few prospects, living in a strange city, a mortgage to feed and family to care for: a two-year-old child, and a baby on the way. Putting the best face on it, one could say that the needs of a burgeoning family life motivated me to new heights of industry. It was like that, and yet it wasn't. It is a quirk of nature that I can, with patience and perseverance, overlook hardship and adversity. My wife cynically calls it shortsighted self-involvement. I prefer to think of it as sublimating my suffering: rendering the dross of travail, as it were, into pure, golden Art.

However it was, when I settled at my desk that day I felt the heady exhilaration of the freelance artist. It is the same thrill I imagine jungle explorers feel – striking off into uncharted territory with only your instincts to protect you from certain disaster. It's high adventure. While you might not be eaten by a cannibal or fall prey to a hideous tropical disease, the peculiar risks of freelance life are real enough.

For example, there is the very ominous and ever-present danger that one's creation will fail and be repudiated, that the beautiful child of one's artistic devotion will fall flat on its chubby little face. There is potential discouragement, rejection, loss. Artistic sensibilities are tender, creative egos fragile. They bruise more easily than bananas.

So, what did I write when I settled before the keyboard that day?

The answer is obvious: I said to myself, 'I shall write a masterwork of heroic fiction after the style of *The Hobbit*! Indeed, I shall swathe myself in the mantle of the Beloved Tolkien and become an author of massive fantasy novels. What is more, the example of the Inklings will become my constant inspiration and my guiding light.'

As much as I might like to remember it that way, the truth is a good deal less high-flown. Utterly mundane, in fact. I really had no idea what I would do that first day. I simply went in to my bedroom office and sat down at the desk, rolled a piece of yellow paper into the typewriter and began typing. If I gave thought at all to what I wanted to do it was simply to write the best and most entertaining story I could. That is, to write a book that I myself would like to read. I figured that if I liked the book then I'd have pleased at least one person.

I did not think in terms of fantasy. I did not think in terms of Great Literature. I did not think in terms of Tolkien. I set out to please myself – Tolkien didn't enter into it.

Now, many people find that extremely odd. I know because I run into these people all the time. They approach me assuming that since I have written a fantasy book or two, I must have a Tolkien shrine in my living room before which I prostrate myself daily. They assume I carry photos of C. S. Lewis in my wallet, and that I've named my children Clive and Bilbo. I must, they think, have committed to memory whole passages of *The Hobbit* and can recite the entire *Chronicles of Narnia* upon request.

It disappoints them to learn the shabby truth: I keep no shrine, I own no autographed first editions, my children do not have a Frodo or Staples between them. I couldn't repeat a scrap of *Dawn Treader* to save my scalp. I have never smoked a pipe.

Yet, the lessons I learned from Lewis and Tolkien penetrated deep into my psyche – deeper than emulation, deeper than imitation. In short, it was not Tolkien's style or subject matter that influenced me; it was the integrity of the work itself.

I found this same integrity in Lewis's space tales. Taken together, these books possessed an inner worth that far exceeded the narrative skills of their authors. *Perelandra* and *The Lord of the Rings* seemed to me more in total than the simple sum of their parts. These books, I concluded, derived their value chiefly from this inner worth, this integrity that lay behind the stories themselves. But what was it?

It was, of course, the Christian faith of the authors shining through the fabric of their work. I saw that faith informed the story, and infused it with value and meaning, lifting the tale above the ordinary expressions of the genre. Even though the stories of Lewis, Tolkien, or other Inklings like Charles Williams, were not explicitly promoting Christianity, nevertheless the books were ripe with it.

What an extraordinary thing, I thought; though Tolkien makes never so much as a glancing reference to Jesus Christ in a single paragraph of all *The Lord of the Rings'* thick volumes, His face is glimpsed on virtually every page. *The Lion, the Witch, and the Wardrobe* is the furthest thing from a religious tract, yet it proclaims a clear and winning gospel. In my narrow experience, I had never before encountered such a thing. How did the authors do that?

That is what I set out to discover. And here is where I had my first surprise: they did not do it on purpose. At least, not as I defined the word. I had assumed that when Christian writers wrote, they entered a process that went something like this:

'Well,' the writer says, 'I have this burning message I must at all costs communicate to a lost and dying world. How shall I then write? I have it! Yes! I shall compose an engaging work of fiction which will subtly, yet ingeniously deliver my life-changing message to the fallen masses who shall read my masterpiece and turn as one to the Light of salvation.'

As an American Christian I came out of a long tradition of nuts-and-bolts pragmatism, a sort of holy practicality that looks upon all things as possible conduits for the Good News. I had it drummed into my head that when it came to the propagation of the gospel, virtually any medium of communication could, and should, become a tool.

I figured this was universally recognized and patently self-evident. I had been taught that if you were a Christian, your first duty was spreading the Good News. Whether you were a banker or a bricklayer, your solitary goal and ambition should be to further the faith by spreading the gospel message in your sphere of life. Certainly, if you were an artist of any sort then your path was fairly well determined: you must use your art.

After all, the logic goes, if tea bags and T-shirts can be pressed into the service of the Great Commission, then certainly Art ought to be. And if communicating the gospel is the primary goal of a Christian, then writing, the most directly communicative form of art, should communicate the gospel most directly.

Relentlessly utilitarian though it may be, that is the evangelical tradition. Perhaps I am perverse. But words like 'ought' and 'should' always make me uncomfortable. They seem to suggest a stern, probably Puritanical disapproval of what *is*. Equally discomforting are words like 'Art' which always seems to connote some sort of immense, fog-bound philosophical abstract of interest only to fatuous snobs and the egg-headed effete.

Yet what I discovered in the pages of Tolkien's *Return of the King*, and Lewis's *Perelandra*, was no mere argument for egg-heads, but a very powerful and persuasive proposition for us all. Put in the smallest nutshell, the proposition, as I understand it, goes like this: Art is a holy entity unto itself, and therefore requires no explicit religious imprimatur to warrant its existence. Art, as the saying goes, needs no justification.

Now, I know this is not a new idea. But I cannot tell you how revolutionary this notion was, and is, to me. I heard in it the thunder of locks exploding and the whine of long-rusted gates swinging open. Ah, freedom!

Freedom, because for me the idea of art as an inherently godly enterprise meant that I did not have to make of my work a disguised sermon, or somehow include the Four Spiritual Laws of Salvation in my story outline, or fuss about right doctrine, or evangelism, or any other parochial religious concern. I was free to pursue my artistic vision wherever it led me, no apologies, no looking fearfully over my shoulder to some imagined arbiter of ecclesiastical approval.

In pretty short order, however, I came to see that this freedom also carried a responsibility (wouldn't you know it?) to practise my art at the highest level of my abilities, to strive for excellence, to make it true. Still, as long as I held true art as my aim, I was free to write as I pleased. The proof was sitting squarely on my bookshelf in four fat volumes by J. R. R. Tolkien.

As I have become persuaded, the most important part of what art does is search for, capture, and offer up to view the three verities: Goodness, Beauty, and Truth. This is the High Quest of art, and Tolkien taught me – no, he showed me – how this quest could be successfully undertaken. I came away convinced that as an artist I had a distinct responsibility, a duty to conduct the quest in my own work.

(That much of modern artistic endeavour has chosen to abandon its duty to the High Quest does not mean that the duty has been revoked. The marching orders have not been rescinded merely because the soldiers have lost their way. That, frankly, is their problem. Mine is to pursue the High Quest to my utmost ability, to search for, capture, and offer up to view Goodness, Beauty, and Truth. This is my calling, yes, but it is the same for anyone else who dares pick up pen or brush or leotard.)

Struggling after Goodness, Beauty, and Truth is, I believe, the only legitimate business of art and artists. If our art tries to do anything else – such as preach or evangelize – it devalues itself and thus falls prey to the same fate awaiting other works whose creators have abandoned the Quest.

So many Christian artists find themselves hung out to dry on the twin horns of that age-old artistic dilemma: Pure Art vs. Propaganda. The Purists dig in at the art-for-art's-sake pole and erect their elitist totems. They declare that art, to be true, must reject all constraints and duties, especially, it seems, the duty of providing a moral message. Meanwhile, half a world away, the Propagandists set up camp in the art-as-means-to-an-end arena. They maintain that the pursuit of pure art is futile because once art has loosed all bonds of duty – such as providing a moral message – it ceases to be true.

I have learned that the path into the heart of that debate is old and thorny, with plenty of pitfalls on either side. The more I worked at threading my way through the conflict, the more treacherous the path became. Better hunters with bigger guns than mine have set out in high hopes of bagging a solution only to come dragging back in dismal defeat.

It was J. R. R. Tolkien who came to my rescue. He showed me a way out of the morass that allowed me to retain my artistic integrity and continue the High Quest without getting impaled on either horn of the unruly dilemma. In the pages of *The Lord of the Rings*, I saw that a judicious balance could be maintained which allowed the artist the cherished freedom to work – without becoming a dreary moralist drudge on the one hand, or a slave to soulless purism on the other.

Tolkien's middle way might be called the Freedom of Implicity. The way I came to see it, the Freedom of Implicity slogan goes something like this: Art, when conscientiously following the High Quest, reveals more of God implicitly than it could any other way – even more than if it had set out to reveal God in the first place!

There is a paradox of sorts at work here. How to explain it? Perhaps it is like a painter who sets out to paint a portrait of God. 'After all,' says he, 'what could be more inspiring and winning than God's beatific image? It will move entire nations to worship and adoration. What more godly purpose for my work could I ask?' So he begins to paint with great religious fervour and zeal.

But he doesn't get very far before he discovers that since no one alive has ever seen the face of the Almighty there are no suitable references – no photographs, no sketches, no graven images of any kind. How then does he paint a portrait of a subject who refuses to give a studio sitting? That is the question: How does one illustrate the invisible?

It cannot be done. At least, it cannot be done explicitly. But an artist can achieve a satisfactory, even extraordinary, result with an implicit approach. That is, he does not paint God directly. Instead, the artist paints the Creator's reflected glory – paints the objects God has touched, the visible trail of his passing, the footprints he leaves behind.

That is precisely what I saw in *The Lord of the Rings*: the visible trail of God's passing, the hallowed glow of his lingering presence. In his massive fantasy epic, Tolkien paints a convincing portrait of Goodness, Beauty, and Truth. His art is true. And insofar as it is true, it is godly. The story of furry-footed hobbits and men struggling to save the world of Middle-earth from the ravages of creeping evil reveals much of God and his redemptive work in this world. Tolkien's creation is a powerful and revealing portrait of the Creator.

What is more, I am convinced that this revelation was no happy accident. Tolkien meant to do it. He worked intentionally and purposefully to that end. Now, on the face of it, this would seem to contradict what I wrote earlier about 'freedom' and 'not doing it on purpose'. Not really. The apparent contradiction is the result of confusing the purpose of the work with the effect achieved.

When I turned the last page of *The Lord of the Rings*, I little guessed that such a stunning and stirring portrait of goodness could be achieved in any way other than by cold-blooded calculation on the part of the author. But I had confused the effect of the work with the purpose of the artist.

And the more I learned about Tolkien, the more I learned that his primary aim as a writer had been to tell an entertaining story – not to preach godliness. This I discovered through his letters.

I lived in Oxford for a time, working on the first volumes of my *Pendragon Cycle*. During that time Blackwells, the ancient and honourable bookstore in the university precinct, hosted a fiftieth anniversary celebration of the publication of *The Hobbit*. As part of the festivities Blackwells put on an exhibit of Tolkien memorabilia, including a sampling of Tolkien's correspondence. I read those letters, and they provided me a first-hand look.

One letter was especially telling. It was written to his publisher following the release of *The Hobbit*, a book greeted with fair success. Naturally, the publisher had inquired whether Professor Tolkien had any more stories about hobbits lying about – if so, they would like to see them, yes they would.

Apparently, Tolkien took his time responding and in the end was forced to write back with a negative answer, saying, 'All the same I am a little perturbed. I cannot think of anything more to say about hobbits.' In another place he wondered, 'What more can hobbits do?' In the end, however, he conceded, 'But if it is true that *The Hobbit* has come to stay and that more will be wanted, I will start the process of thought, and try to get some idea of a theme drawn from this material ...' He goes on to express his 'faint hope' that his writing will begin to loosen the financial constraints he has laboured under for many years so that he can devote more time to his work.

There was no mention of purpose or message, no hint of any explicit didactic purpose at all. This letter and others I have read reveal Tolkien's primary concern: to find and tell a good story. Indeed, *The Hobbit* began as a bedtime tale for his children's entertainment. Likewise, on evidence of the letters, *The Lord of the Rings* began as a simple response to supply the publisher with another book – more from a financial motive than any other, as I read it.

Don't blanch at such a pragmatic motive. What matters isn't what motivates a writer to sit down at his desk; it is what the writer does once he gets there. What Tolkien actually did when he put pen to paper was nothing less than create a whole new class of literature: heroic fantasy.

Say the word 'fantasy' in a crowded room and alarm bells go off. I know, because I get letters from these alarmed individuals all the time by virtue of my work. For them, the words fiction and lies are synonymous, with not a nickel's worth of difference between them. Since by definition fiction is not factual documentary, fiction is therefore false. Anything false is a lie. All lies are evil. Ergo: fiction is evil. And the most suspicious fiction of all is (snarl, snarl) escapist fantasy.

Escape! To many people the term 'escapist fantasy' connotes frivolity, sensuality, idleness, and unreality – hardly healthy involvements for hard-headed, feet-on-the-solid-ground, no-nonsense, just-the-facts Christians.

Tolkien had to face this same attitude; in his day, he was accused of writing an escapist literature which would lead people to abandon reality in favour of an impossibly rich and exciting imaginary life. Tolkien's response was unequivocal: 'Yes,' he declared, 'fantasy is escapist, and that is its glory. If a soldier is imprisoned by the enemy, don't we consider it his duty to escape? The moneylenders, the know-nothings, the authoritarians have us all in prison; if we value the freedom of the mind and soul, if we're partisans of liberty, then it's our plain duty to escape, and to take as many people with us as we can!'

In that pithy pronouncement I heard once again the sound of those prison doors swinging open. Tolkien brilliantly deflects the objection by admitting the truth of the observation. And he goes on to say that since fantasy is escapist, it makes little difference what you are escaping *from*, but a very great deal of difference what you are escaping *to*. For the best of fantasy offers not an escape away from reality, but an escape to a heightened reality – a world at once more vivid and intense and real, where happiness and sorrow exist in double measure, where good and evil war in epic conflict, where joy is made more potent by the possibility of universal tragedy and defeat.

In the very best fantasy literature, like *The Lord of the Rings*, we escape into an ideal world where ideal heroes and heroines (who are really only parts of our truer selves) behave ideally. The work describes human life as it might be lived, perhaps ought to be lived, against a backdrop, not of all happiness and light, but of crushing difficulty and overwhelming distress. It is this modelling of behaviour which nourishes and strengthens the inner child in all of us. And, unless I am very much mistaken, this same inner child is who we will become when the mortal flesh melts away, and we enter the life eternal.

Yes, fantasy is escapist. The spiritual journey of the soul is not easily rendered in terms of the ultra-rational, ultra-realistic. But it is natural to the escapist medium of fantasy, Tolkien maintained. And he might have added as an aside to well-intentioned Christians that Christianity itself is a venture founded on the conviction that escape is good for the soul. What is salvation, if not escape?

We hope, through our faith in Christ, to escape the death penalty which sin has decreed. It seems to me that fantasy literature actually mirrors this great hope in its fundamental design. Perhaps it is enough that it does so. But, when the mirror of fantasy is polished bright by a master storyteller engaged in the High Quest, it becomes, like Alice in Wonderland's mirror, not a mirror only, but also a window to another world. A world which is really our own world lovingly created anew.

The world of the author's creation is offered up to the delight of the reader, and because he delights he entertains. And because he entertains, all sorts of things become possible. An entertained person is a receptive person, open to the unfolding experience, open to taking in something of the artist's vision. It is all to the good if that vision is true and godly.

Tolkien demonstrates this process absolutely. In his tale of Frodo, Strider, Gandalf, and their beautiful, magical world of Middle-earth, Professor Tolkien masterfully illustrates the tremendous power of True Art to inspire, enlighten, ennoble, challenge, and persuade, not to mention entertain – which was, after all, Tolkien's primary purpose.

Back at my desk, toiling away to master the power of implicity in my work, I began to get a grip on it at last. As I wrestled my way through the *Dragon King Trilogy* and then *Empyrion* I and II and on into the *Pendragon Cycle*, I learned that there was a greater force at work here than I first realized. I mentioned before that I thought Tolkien had set out to make his work godly on purpose. As usual, I had it backwards. He set out purposefully to make his art true. And because he succeeded, it became godly.

Stating it like that may make the process sound a bit random or haphazard, but there is nothing at all arbitrary about it. Tolkien worked at his art in a very exacting, methodical way, according to a philosophy of literature which he had developed – a philosophy his friend C. S. Lewis called the 'Tolkienian Theory of Sub-creation'. According to this theory, the artist is a creator working in exactly the same way as God the Creator works; the artist becomes a mini-creator, his world a sub-created world reflecting God's creation.

In the final analysis, that is precisely what fantasy literature is: a celebration of life in all its myriad elements. It is nothing less than a praise hymn to creation, and its melody runs through all fantasy literature. Even the shabbiest fantasy pulp novel contains strains of it. No other entertainment form that I know of is so constructed on this premise, this fundamental recognition of the holiness of creation. It is basic to the enterprise. In fact, the fundamental act of writing the fantasy novel requires a strict acknowledgement of the basic beauty and immanent goodness of God's creation by the author. The sub-created world becomes an extension of the Divine Presence.

I do not suggest that every writer of fantasy consciously receives his work in just this way. I suppose many, perhaps most, do not. Tolkien himself worked blindly much of the time. The agonizing process by which his masterwork came to be written is detailed in the collection of his letters, where, after twelve years of difficult gestation, he writes to the publisher in utter shock and dismay at what he has created. 'I am, I fear, a most unsatisfactory person,' Tolkien announced bleakly. 'Now I look at it, the magnitude of the disaster is apparent to me. My work has escaped from my control, and I have produced a monster: an immensely long, complex, rather bitter, and very terrifying romance, quite unfit for children (if fit for anybody).'

Tolkien was happily mistaken. The author is quite often the last to know what has transpired through him. Certainly, many writers with far less integrity than Tolkien remain blissfully oblivious to the High Quest all their lives. But that does not change the level of their participation in this holy scheme. A God who is capable of wringing shouts of joy from the rocks beneath our feet ought to be able to move a few myopic fantasy hacks to hum a snatch of harmony.

In the very best of fantasy literature the hymn of praise can achieve quite astonishing heights – something on the order of a psalm become symphony. Certainly, in *The Lord of the Rings* we glimpse such a transformation. Tolkien was a master and worked very hard at his art; he also worked from a detailed understanding of his craft. For Tolkien, the creation and exploration of fantasy worlds were a way of examining the image of the Maker as revealed in his creation and in his creatures. It was also a way of probing the nature of the Fall and the tremendous grace and power manifest in the Incarnation and Redemption. Fantasy, like all True Art, becomes a kind of extended parable by which hidden facets of the multi-dimensional reality of life are illumined.

That it often does so in an extremely entertaining manner is, some would say, something of a plus, a serendipitous extra. But I disagree. In fact, it is much the other way around.

Entertainment, you will remember, was for Tolkien the original intent and purpose.

Tolkien set out to entertain with his stories – his own children first, and then others. But in the telling, the stories grew into something far grander than anything he himself imagined when he began. That is always the best way. The writer begins with little more than the thread of an idea and the desire to follow it and see where it will go. But as he works at his creation, his labour becomes a sacrifice, of his time if nothing else (but most often, of much else besides). And if he is faithful to the High Quest, God, I believe, accepts the sacrifice and enters into it in ways unforeseen by even the author himself.

Though I make no claim to Tolkien's mantle, I have written enough imaginative fiction to know something of how it was for him. For I have seen the same things happen in my own work. My main purpose as a writer of popular fiction has always been to entertain. That is, after all, the reason people read popular fiction in the first place. But, as I have struggled to remain true to the High Quest, I have seen the narrative take some very surprising twists: events and characters resonating with deeper meaning; nuances of relevance highlighted; truth, beauty, and goodness startlingly revealed. And all in ways that I could not have contrived with all my might, even on a very good day.

But then, is that not God's job? It is God who takes our meagre sacrifices and transforms them into blessings – a few loaves and fishes into a feast for thousands! My job, I keep reminding myself, is to follow the High Quest to the best of my ability, to make the daily sacrifice, and let God take it from there. Tolkien has taught me that. And if I never write anything remotely approaching his monumental achievement, still I will have done my part.

13

THE PASSION ACCORDING TO TOLKIEN
SEAN MCGRATH

Sean McGrath, a native of Newfoundland, wrote this essay as a special feature in the Winter 1992 edition of Desert Call *(now published as* Forefront*), the journal of the Carmelite Community in Colorado. Father Dave Denny,* Forefront's *editor, writes: 'In 1994, the Spiritual Life Institute, publisher of* Desert Call, *renamed the quarterly magazine. Now titled* Forefront: the Desert and the City, *this journal of contemplation and culture is available from The Spiritual Life Institute, PO Box 219, Crestone, CO 81131, USA. Phone: 719-256-4778. Fax: 719-256-4719.'*

It is a common misconception to think of the cross as something entirely alien to Christ imposed on him by an ugly necessity, call it original sin or the problem of evil. But we have his own words to refute such a view. When his disciples squirmed uncomfortably as he described what must transpire at Golgotha if he was to fulfil his end he assured them, 'No one takes my life from me. I lay it down of my own accord. I have the power to lay it down, and the power to take it up again.' Yet Jesus was neither a nihilist nor a suicide. He understood the hunger for life. Indeed he felt we were not hungry enough for it. More than once in the Gospel we see him fighting for his life, hiding out, protecting himself from the machinations of the priests and the Romans. What then was he trying to teach us by his voluntary submission to the horrible fate of crucifixion? That unless a grain of wheat fall and die it remains only a single grain, but if it die it yields a rich harvest; that the transformation from a tiny seed into a stalk of golden wheat has a price: annihilation. Annihilation of our present state of existence is the condition of the possibility of transformation.

What an unfathomable mystery this is; what dizzying paradox; what superhuman trust – that the hunger for life should compel us to choose death! God is the abyss, always beckoning to us, urging us to stretch beyond our limitations, our comfortable familiar perimeters, to explode our present state of incompleteness and receive new form, new substance. When the time was right Jesus knew that he had to do something unprecedented. He had to show the world something even more precious than life as we know it: the unfathomable will of God. His task was to become the sign that men could trust the mysterious purposes of the universe, which often appear hostile and indifferent to our survival. Jesus had to show by his death and resurrection that the cosmos is geared to our enlargement. Like the bronze serpent that Moses lifted up in the desert so that all who looked upon it could be saved, Jesus made himself a living standard. More than merely a symbol he became on the hill of Calvary the first Sacrament, a symbol that is what it signifies. For the death of Christ not only signifies the power of transformation at work in the universe; it is his power.

Before we cheer Jesus' resurrection too loudly we must remember the cost. Death is real. Christianity does not teach a doctrine of immortality in the sense of 'unending existence'. Our present state of existence has an end. The voluntary diminishment we are commanded to choose in the Cross is a real diminishment. We will lose what we have come to cherish as our self, what Daniel Day Williams describes as the 'objective self – the deposit of experience as shaped by our self-understanding'. In other words all that we are most familiar with, the cumulative sum and substance of our conscious life which we cling to desperately as our mistaken identity. The Spirit draws us to the borders of this selfhood, towards transformation which *must* first appear as the abyss, as a great ominous nothingness. For we are being transformed into that which we are not, into that which we know not, even as a glimmer of potency. Absolute renunciation and detachment is required. The Spirit cries to us where we crouch frightened in lesser dimensions of being, 'Jump! Forget what you know or think you know. Forget what you are or think you are. Become something new, something unforeseen, something wonderful. Die!' Nikos Kazantzakis, in his violent, passionate extremism touches the raw nerve of this dynamic at the heart of all creation:

> Blowing through heaven and earth, and in our hearts, and the heart of every living thing, is a gigantic breath – a great cry which we call God. Plant life wished to continue its motionless sleep next to stagnant waters, but the cry leaped up within it and violently shook its roots: 'Away, let go of the earth, walk!' Had the tree been able to think and judge, it would have cried, 'I don't want to. What are you urging me to do! You are demanding the impossible!' But the Cry without pity, kept shaking its roots and shouting, 'Away, let go of the earth, walk!'
>
> The human being is a centaur; his equine hoofs are planted on the ground, but his body from breast to head is worked on and tormented by the merciless Cry. He has been fighting again for thousands of eons to draw himself like a sword, out of his animalistic scabbard. He is also fighting – this is a new struggle – to draw himself out of his human scabbard. Man calls in despair, 'Where can I go? I have reached the pinnacle, beyond is the abyss.' And the Cry answers, 'I am beyond.' (*Report to Greco*, pp. 278–9)

The abyss is terrifyingly real, all-consuming, devoid of light and meaning. Into it goes every human hope, expectation and desire. In its centre it is pure night, the soul-numbing terror of the absurd. It takes from us even the consolation of the tragic. It swallows and annihilates. Nothing that goes into it ever emerges. This death that is the condition of transformation is an annihilation. Standing at the centre of the void is the cross of contradiction promising us – in flagrant denial of the emptiness in which it lies mired – that crucifixion is the highest accomplishment of our humanity, the fullest possible enlargement of our natural beings into supernature. For upon it rides the clown Christ laughing, untouched by despair, transformed through suffering into God.

In a letter J. R. R. Tolkien tells a friend that the central theme of *The Lord of the Rings* is the temptation to immorality. The immortality that the main characters must renounce is the vague but very real natural omnipotence offered them by use of the Dark Lord's Ring of Power. In their quest to destroy it the heroes of the trilogy – Bilbo, Frodo, Aragorn, Gandalf, Sam and Galadriel – all face the temptation to use the power of the Ring to inflate their present state of being beyond all decency and make themselves into a Dark Lord, all-powerful and immortal. Thus their quest to destroy this possibility is a surrender of themselves, a renunciation of the hope of immortality, a quest for death. This comes clear in Galadriel's moment of trial where for an instant she fantasizes at the possibilities opened to her should she choose the Ring over death:

> 'You will give me the Ring freely! In place of the Dark Lord you will set up a queen. And I shall not be dark, but beautiful and terrible as the morning and the night! Fair as the sea and the sun and the snow upon the mountain! Dreadful as the storm and the lightning! Stronger than the foundations of the earth. All shall love me and despair!'

She lifted up her hand and from the ring she wore there issued a great light that illuminated her alone and left all else dark. She stood there before Frodo seeming now tall beyond measurement and beautiful beyond enduring, terrible and worshipful. Then she let her hand fall, and the light faded and suddenly she laughed again, and lo! she was shrunken: a slender elf woman, clad in simple white, whose voice was soft and sad.

'I pass the test. I will diminish and go into the West.' (*Fellowship of the Ring*, pp. 474–5)

Taking the Ring and using its power to extend our present selfhood into deathless perpetuity has its analogue in every act, no matter how trivial, that refuses change in favour of personal aggrandizement. We cannot help but want to preserve ourselves, and our unconscious resistance to death is inculpable. But as we grow increasingly aware of what God requires of us, we grow freer, and our culpability for resisting the edict to be transformed increases. It turns from instinct to sin:

So long as we aim at the maintenance of this present self, as we now conceive it, we cannot enter the larger selfhood which is pressing for life. The natural resistance of the self to becoming is not itself a sin. It is a self-protective device of the human spirit; but when it becomes an invitation to use our freedom against the risk of becoming, it is a temptation to sin. The meaning of sin is usually not that we try to make ourselves the centre of everything. We make our present state of selfhood the meaning of existence, and thus refuse the deeper meaning which lies within and beyond this present. When that refusal becomes refusal to trust in the giver of life and the greater community he is creating, it is a sin. (Daniel Day Williams: *The Spirit and Forms of Love*)

The Lord of the Rings' myth depicts the dynamics of this fundamental option to give up our lives for the sake of a higher good, that lies at the heart of human ethics. The pretty poison that lures us away from God's design towards a kind of temporary personal omnipotence is subtler than the evil at work in Middle-earth. In my daily life in middle-class North America, no winged Nazgûl block out the sun with their huge black wings; no emaciated Sméagols remind us of the price of unchecked selfishness; or do they? This 'escapist' literature presents in vivid dramatic pictures what is otherwise intangible and inexpressible: our battle for salvation, for overcoming the all-pervasive, crippling legacy of sin. It gives form and substance to our very real quest and projects it into an imaginary universe where the ultimate questions are blazingly clear, as clear as the morning sun shining on polished armour, and black banners against the sky.

The false self takes shape before the reader's eyes and assumes an archetypal form that we instinctively recognize as an accurate depiction of our darker side. His name is Sméagol, but all call him Gollum for the hideous sound he makes in the throat. He is a pathetic, snivelling residue of a life starved by its own selfishness, thoroughly repulsive, and deadly.

The reader also meets his hidden dignity, his Christ-self, in the figure of Aragorn, the once and future King, who lives only to serve even though he is spurned and shunned out of fear by those he serves. Here in Middle-earth, against the magnificent pageantry of a world as fresh and inexhaustibly fascinating as ours once was, our individual quest for death is given the scale it deserves; upon its success hangs the fate of the entire world.

And here, in Frodo's agonizing pilgrimage to Mordor and the cracks of Doom the depth of our sacrifice is at last adequately portrayed. For when God asks us to transcend our present state of being he is asking us to break and spend ourselves as relentlessly as Frodo gives his entire being to the quest. Daniel Day Williams's theological language does not convey the agony of this breaking. Kazantzakis in *St Francis* comes closer to the explosive emotions involved in surrendering to transformation:

> Listen to what I shall call Him: the Bottomless Abyss, the Insatiable, the Merciless, the Indefatigable, the Unsatisfied. He who never once said to poor unfortunate mankind 'Enough!'
> 'Not enough,' that is what he screamed at me.
> 'I can't go further,' whines miserable man.
> 'You can!' the Lord replies.
> 'I shall break in two,' man whines again.
> 'Break!'

The wizard Gandalf's death and resurrection is the supreme enactment of this drama of surrender, annihilation, and transformation. The threshold of transformation is always the experience of one's limitations. We come up against the borders of our limited being and we know that death is the only way through and beyond. In the novel the company of the Ring, led by the wizard, comes to a dead halt at the impassable snow-blasted mountain Caradhras. The only way beyond is through the long-abandoned Mines of Moria which tunnel beneath the rock. Aragorn instinctively knows that something terrible will befall the company if they enter Moria, and though unsure of the shape it will take, he senses an imminent danger to the wizard. Gandalf, however, is unyielding. His cause is with the success of the quest, and though he doubtlessly knows that Aragorn's premonition is true, he insists that they continue. The ensuing stand-off reminds us of Peter trying to dissuade Christ from taking his Cross. For Gandalf must know that he will die in Moria; one doesn't get to be a wizard for nothing! Yet he also knows that the company will get through without him, and is willing, indeed eager to pay the price. His disaffected fellow wizard Saruman preceded him to this spot, the brink of transformation, and failed, turned away, chose self-aggrandizement over diminishment. Gandalf will not make the same mistake. So the aged wizard leads the company into the mines where he meets his doom, the Balrog, which drags him into the abyss from whence he never returns. Out of the apocalyptic battle emerges something entirely new and brilliant, born of the ashes of his sacrifice: the White Rider.

> 'Gandalf!' Gimli said. 'But you are all in white!'
>
> 'Gandalf,' the old man repeated as if recalling from old memory a long disused word. 'Yes, that was my name. I was Gandalf. Yes, you may still call me Gandalf. I am white now. Indeed I am Saruman one might almost say, Saruman as he should have been.' (The Two Towers, p. 119)

The temptation to power intensifies the pain of sacrifice. Galadriel for a moment is enticed by the possibilities of such power, of herself enlarged to mammoth proportions, capable at last of imposing her 'benign' will on Middle-earth. Saruman chose 'many colours' over the stark purity of the white robe, and for a while he possesses power, even over Gandalf. There is power and temporary satisfaction in sin. We can choose to use the freedom for our own immediate ends and experience a momentary gratification. How else do we account for the problem of evil? In Eternity, however, such power is so infinitesimal as to be non-existent, a chimera of life, a pale distorted reflection of Reality. To take up the Ring is to place oneself outside of God, in true nothingness. Thus the 'Nine Men Doomed to Die' who chose the Ring over death became wraiths, insubstantial shadows. Saruman by the end of the book has degenerated into a weak, spiteful dabbler in petty evil who is stabbed to death by his own servant. His desire for life without death has placed him so far outside the Real that he is almost insubstantial, and disperses like a plume of smoke when stabbed. This is hardly death, but rather the final stages of decomposition that began with his real death long before, when he chose power over transformation. The apogee of this deep metaphysical truth – the truth that evil, which is the desire for being apart from God, is unreal, empty negation, progressively poorer in being the further it moves from the Divine Will – is the Dark Lord himself who is utterly bodiless, evanescent; a disincarnate hatred, seen only in nightmares as a lidless eye.

The heroes of *The Lord of the Rings* who choose death mysteriously, yet unmistakably, increase in reality. This is the central paradox of the mystical life: diminishment in natural being is not necessarily a diminishment of Reality, but is rather often accompanied by a profound intensification of life presence. One thinks of the elderly, or the sick, who, through acceptance of fate, have made it their own and are lit up from within with a holy presence. In the myth Gandalf is again the obvious example. Yet a subtler display of this mysterious ontological deepening appears in the case of Boromir's self-sacrifice which was not so clearly brought to the glory of resurrection. His finest hour comes when he falls defending the hobbits. As he lies dying against the tree, his proud heart filled with arrow-heads, he confesses that he fell to the temptation of the Ring and tried to wrest it from Frodo. He clearly wins a mighty victory over death and achieves a deep level of reality. King Théoden is another shining example, crumpling in glory beneath the black wings of the Nazgûl with the battle cry of his Rohirrim raging about him. We know that this is more of a man than the one who sat pining and sinking in his throne, poisoned with fear and attachment, and robbed of all energy and vitality.

With Frodo's quest for death achieved in the fire of Mount Doom, the metaphysical dynamic at play in all the dying required of us in the mystical life is brought to the fore. For it is not Frodo that falls into the fire but his ego: Gollum, the personification of his false self, wretched, miserable, hating life and light. Frodo achieves his quest on Mount Doom and so does Gollum, who at last is united with the Ring's unholy power and falls screaming into the volcano's fiery chasm. Here is a mighty secret: the shadow, the false self, lends us the rage to carry out the final emancipation. In spite of himself, his hate is channelled into obedience to a higher plan and becomes the catalyst of transformation. Gollum serves Frodo until the bitter end much as Judas remains in Jesus' company; because his hate, his violence, plays a crucial role in the outcome. We don't have it in us – in our conscious socialized ego – to hurl ourselves into the abyss. We need a prod from the darker, unpleasant dimensions of our being that we instinctively recoil from.

In the end Frodo, now changed to be sure, no longer the comfort-loving hobbit who sat by his fire in his beloved Shire, dreading all thought of leaving his safe, cosy hearth, passes into the Eternal West with those other titans of the Spirit: Galadriel, Bilbo, Gandalf, those who risked all and paid the price. They pass into that Life that is ours if only we will let go of all lesser forms of existence. For how can God, who is incapable of cruelty, and who so values human freedom that he is willing to pay the price of all suffering – how can he change that which refuses to change, and transform that which does not want new form? He cannot. He is bound by his own infinite goodness to permit evil for a time, which is nothing more than the empty negation of his intentions, empty because evil has nothing to put in their place.

Christianity teaches the inescapability, finality, and even desirability of death. But it is neither pessimistic nor nihilistic. The life we cling to and refuse to part with even when God himself commands that we let it go, is no life at all. It is a shadow of the sheer bounty of being we are meant for. The Quester for Life whose quest leads him to choose death is a distinctively Christian archetype. In the Classical World, the quest for life led to an aversion to death and corruptibility and a longing for an eternity of the natural: Olympus. And what else could the unaided human imagination describe as the ultimate good of man? It was only with Christ and his incredible Cross that the mystery pulsating at the heart of life and death was unveiled. The pagan love for life is surely the beginning. But it must be exponentially multiplied until it absorbs even our fear of death.

14

THE OTHER OXFORD MOVEMENT:
TOLKIEN AND THE INKLINGS
WALTER HOOPER

Walter Hooper's article on the Inklings first appeared in the June 1997 issue of Catholic World Report.

The Oxford Movement began in 1833 under the leadership of John Keble, E. B. Pusey, and John Henry Newman. These churchmen had in mind a return of the Anglican Communion to a 'Catholic' Church faithful to the Early Fathers and free of undue influence from governments. The movement reached its climax in 1845 with Newman's conversion to Catholicism.

Another movement which began in Oxford a century later and which has given us shelves of great books is that of the Inklings. This group of Christian friends, most of whom taught at Oxford University, included C. S. Lewis, J. R. R. Tolkien, and Owen Barfield. They met weekly in Lewis's rooms in Magdalen College to talk, drink, and read aloud whatever any of them was writing. They gathered as well on Tuesday mornings over beer and pipes in the Eagle and Child pub, or the 'Bird and Baby' as it is known. Visitors to Oxford can usually find a seat in the snug little back room of the 'Bird and Baby' where photographs and other mementos of the Inklings are displayed.

When you are settled with a drink, you'll probably ask 'Why did they call themselves Inklings? How did it all begin?' The first question was answered by Tolkien, who explained that they were 'people with vague or half-formed intimations and ideas plus those who dabble in ink'.

They began with C. S. Lewis and his passion for hearing things read aloud. The first to share this with him was Owen Barfield. They met at Oxford in 1919 when both were undergraduates. Lewis loved 'rational opposition' and Barfield supplied plenty of this. Besides sharing the same interests, Lewis wrote in *Surprised by Joy*, Barfield was 'approaching them all at a different angle'.

'When you set out to correct his heresies,' said Lewis, 'you find he forsooth has decided to correct yours! And then you go at it, hammer and tongs, far into the night ... out of this perpetual dogfight a community of mind and a deep affection emerge.' Barfield compared arguing with Lewis to 'wielding a peashooter against a howitzer'. It must be understood that 'rational opposition' is not quarrelling. 'We were always,' said Barfield, 'arguing for truth not for victory, and arguing for truth, not for comfort.' Before he moved to London in 1930 to work as a solicitor, Barfield published *Poetic Diction* (1928), a work that was to have a profound influence on the other Inklings.

Lewis's next great friend was J. R. R. Tolkien. They met in 1926, each having joined the English faculty of Oxford University the year before, Lewis as Fellow of English at Magdalen College and Tolkien as Professor of Anglo-Saxon. 'At my first coming into the world,' Lewis said in *Surprised by Joy*, 'I had been (implicitly) warned never to trust a Papist, and at my first coming into the English Faculty (explicitly) never to trust a philologist. Tolkien was both.' The friendship nevertheless grew quickly, and soon Tolkien was going to Lewis's college rooms on Monday mornings where he read aloud some of *The Silmarillion*, early stories about his huge mythological world of 'Middle-earth'.

It was Lewis's grandfathers who warned him against the Papists, and it is interesting to imagine what they would have thought of the debt their grandson would one day owe this particular Catholic. Lewis became an atheist when he was fourteen as a result of finding that all teachers and editors of the Classics took it for granted that the beliefs of the pagans were 'a mere farrago of nonsense'. As they did not attempt to show how Christianity fulfilled paganism or how paganism prefigured Christianity, Lewis concluded that Christianity was equally nonsensical.

Then came an evening in Magdalen College, 19 September 1931, that was to be the most momentous of his life. Lewis invited Tolkien and Hugo Dyson, a teacher at Reading University, to dine. By the time Tolkien left Magdalen at 3 a.m. Lewis understood the relationship between Christianity and paganism. 'What Dyson and Tolkien showed me,' he wrote to Arthur Greeves on 18 October 1931,

> was that the idea of a dying and reviving god ... moved me provided I met it anywhere except in the gospels ... Now the story of Christ is simply a true myth: a myth working on us in the same way as the others, but with this tremendous difference that it *really happened*: and one must be content to accept it in the same way, remembering that it is God's myth where the others are men's myths: i.e. the Pagan stories are God expressing Himself through the minds of the poets, using such images as He found there, while Christianity is God expressing Himself through what we call 'real things' ... namely, the actual incarnation, crucifixion, and resurrection.

From this point on Lewis became a muscular defender of those 'real things'.

About this same time an undergraduate at University College, Edward Tangye Lean, formed a club actually called 'The Inklings'. Its members met for the very purpose of reading aloud unpublished compositions, and Lewis and Tolkien were invited to join. The club died when Lean took his degree and left Oxford in 1933, and Lewis and Tolkien then transferred its name to their group in Magdalen.

The foundations of the Inklings were now in place. Lewis's brother, Warnie, attended the occasional meeting when he was home from the Army, and they were often joined by Barfield and Hugo Dyson. Then on 4 February 1933 Lewis wrote excitedly to Arthur Greeves: 'Since term began I have had a delightful time reading a children's story which Tolkien has just written.' It was *The Hobbit* (1937), the first work by an Inkling to become a classic.

From there Lewis and Tolkien went on to plan a joint project. They were dissatisfied with much of what they found in stories, and Lewis suggested that they each write one of their own. They had in mind stories that were 'mythopoeic' – having the quality of myth – but disguised as thrillers. Tolkien wrote *The Lost Road*, the story of a journey back through time.

Lewis saw this as an opportunity to put into effect one of the things that was to be a hallmark of his writing. It is a 'supposal' – suppose there are rational creatures on other planets that are unfallen? Suppose we meet them? 'I liked the whole interplanetary idea,' he said, 'as a mythology and simply wished to conquer for my own (Christian) point of view what has always hitherto been used by the opposite side.' The result was his novel *Out of the Silent Planet* (1938), in which the adventurers from Earth discover on Malacandra (Mars) three races of beings who have never Fallen, and are not in need of redemption because they are obedient to Maleldil (God). When some of his readers failed to see what he was 'getting at', he concluded that 'any amount of theology can now be smuggled into people's minds under cover of romance without their knowing it'. Some years later the Inklings were treated to another of Lewis's 'supposals' in the *Chronicles of Narnia*. *The Lion, the Witch and the Wardrobe* was, he said, an answer to the question 'Supposing there was a world like Narnia, and supposing, like ours, it needed redemption, let us imagine what sort of Incarnation and Passion and Resurrection Christ would have there.'

While Lewis was still writing *Out of the Silent Planet*, Tolkien began his masterpiece *The Lord of the Rings*, which was read and discussed during many meetings of the Inklings. This work cannot be separated from one of Tolkien's most important literary theories – that of 'sub-creation' which he wrote about in his essay 'On Fairy Stories'. According to Tolkien, while Man was disgraced by the Fall and for a long time estranged from God, he is not wholly lost or changed from his original nature. He retains the likeness of his Maker. Man shows that he is made in the image and likeness of the Maker when, acting in a 'derivative mode', he writes stories which reflect the eternal Beauty and Wisdom. Imagination is 'the power of giving to ideal creations the inner consistency of reality'. When Man draws things from the Primary World and creates a Secondary World he is acting as a 'sub-creator'. His sub-creations may have several effects. Man needs to be freed from the drab blur of triteness, familiarity, and possessiveness which impair his sight, and such stories help him recover 'a clear view' of the Creation. Another effect is the 'Consolation of the Happy Ending' or *eucatastrophe*. Such stories do not deny the existence of sorrow and failure, but they provide 'a sudden glimpse of the underlying reality or truth'. After all, the Gospel or *evangelium* contains 'a story of a larger kind which embraces all the essence of fairy stories'. In God's kingdom we must not imagine that the presence of the greatest depresses the small. The *evangelium* has not destroyed stories, but hallowed them, especially those with the 'happy ending'.

The Second World War caused a huge upheaval in Oxford. Most of the Inklings had served in the First War but they could not be sure they would be left alone this time. Warnie Lewis was recalled to active service in 1939, and now, in retrospect, it is clear that the war years were the Inklings' golden age. The many new members who joined during these years included Lord David Cecil, lecturer in English at New College; Nevill Coghill, English tutor at Exeter College; James Dundas-Grant, Commander of the Oxford University Naval Division; Adam Fox, Dean of Divinity at Magdalen; Colin Hardie, Classical tutor at Magdalen; R. E. 'Humphrey' Havard, Lewis's doctor; R. B. McCallum of Pembroke College; Father Gervase Mathew OP, of Blackfriars; C. E. Stevens, historian at Magdalen; Charles Wrenn, lecturer in English Language; Christopher Tolkien (son of JRRT) and John Wain, both students at the time. Of the new members perhaps the one who had the greatest influence on Lewis was Charles Williams, an employee of Oxford University Press, who was evacuated with the Press to Oxford.

Lewis was a fervent admirer of Williams's 'theological thrillers' beginning with *The Place of the Lion*. Other friends such as George Sayer and Roger Lancelyn Green dropped in when they were visiting Oxford.

It was rare for all these men to be at every meeting, and some who could not get to the evening gatherings were present at the 'Bird and Baby' on Tuesday mornings. The Thursday evening meetings in Lewis's rooms began about 9 a.m., and describing them in *Sprightly Running* John Wain said:

> I can see the room so clearly now, the electric fire pumping heat into the dank air, the faded screen that broke some of the keener draughts, the enamel beer-jug on the table, the well-worn sofa and armchairs, and the men drifting in ... leaving overcoats and hats in any corner and coming over to warm their hands before finding a chair. There was no fixed etiquette, but the rudimentary honours would be done partly by Lewis and partly by his brother ... Sometimes, when the less vital members of the circle were in a big majority the evening would fall flat; but the best of them were as good as anything I shall live to see.

It was in this setting that, along with lively talk about many things, and without an iota of self-consciousness about securing a place in history, Tolkien's *The Lord of the Rings*, C. S. Lewis's *The Problem of Pain*, *The Screwtape Letters*, and *The Great Divorce*, Charles Williams's *All Hallows' Eve*, and Warnie Lewis's *The Splendid Century* were – along with other works by other members – read and discussed. Those of us who did not enjoy the privilege of being there can at least imagine what it must have been like to read one's own work to such a friendly but formidable jury.

We must not think of the Inklings as anything like a 'mutual admiration society' or men hungry for professional advancement. They were, first and foremost, Christians, who had in common something that was far more important than their jobs or their other interests. Nowhere is this better put than in the definition Lewis gave of Friendship in *The Four Loves*: 'In this kind of love, "*Do you love me?*" means "Do you see the same truth?" or at least, "Do you care about the same truth?"' If Cardinal Newman had been alive at the time, this was the club in which he would have felt at home.

15

TOLKIEN AND C. S. LEWIS:
AN INTERVIEW WITH WALTER HOOPER

Walter Hooper was C. S. Lewis's personal secretary during Lewis's last years. He is now literary adviser to the Lewis estate and, besides editing many volumes of Lewis's writing, is the author of C. S. Lewis: A Companion and Guide. *Mr Hooper also knew Tolkien very well throughout the 1960s so he is uniquely placed to offer an insight into Tolkien's and Lewis's contemporary relevance. This interview was given to Joseph Pearce at Mr Hooper's home in Oxford in April 1998.*

When and where did you first meet Tolkien?

I met Tolkien in the first or second week of January 1964. Before that, when I was with Lewis in his house, The Kilns, in the summer of 1963, he asked me to ring Tolkien and he was very keen that we meet. I rang Tolkien but he said that his wife was not very well and that he couldn't come. Lewis was very disappointed, not only because he wanted to see him again but because he wanted us to meet. I think he wanted to see us meet. Now Tolkien did come to see Lewis several times before Lewis died that autumn, and he certainly didn't abandon him in his last days, but I wasn't present on these occasions.

In any event, after Lewis died and I had returned to Oxford I got in touch with Tolkien and he invited me to his house which was in Sandfield Road. At that time he was using his garage as a very cosy study and he invited me to sit down and he was very nice, he could not have been warmer. Of all the friends of Lewis whom I had met by that time, he was the one who I think was most sympathetic with my plight. He said several times, 'I know it must be so hard on you', and I thought later how he had known Lewis so much longer, for many more years than I had, and yet he knew what Lewis meant to me, he just sensed it. He was a deeply sympathetic man, and this was why, I think, he saw me and why he was so gracious and kind.

When I arrived he had said that the length of the meeting was to be half an hour. He had so many demands on his time that he had to do this. Of course, that meant half an hour to me but I realized of course that he was not constrained by his own rules. I had my eyes on my watch and after half an hour I said 'Thank you very much' and made to leave, but he said 'No, no, no, keep your seat, keep your seat.' We talked about Jack Lewis and one of the points he made was that Lewis 'had not made enough time for me' and I explained that Lewis's view was that Tolkien had not made enough time for him. I think he felt then that it was a pity that they had both claimed to be very busy, which they doubtless were, but you just don't really believe your friends will die.

At the end of our meeting, which must have lasted over an hour because he kept making me sit down, he took me to the gate and he said that I should feel free to contact him at any time and that he was so sorry for the grief I must be feeling. Then I thought how extraordinary it was. He had lost one of his oldest friends and yet he had seen right into the real depths of me in a very particular way. I think, in fact, that he saw deeper into human feelings than Lewis did, perhaps because he was a married man. I liked Mrs Tolkien very much and I found that she had a deep sympathy with anyone who had any sort of problem. I think that she may have been responsible for the fact that Tolkien did care so much for people's feelings. Lewis, on the other hand, much preferred to listen to what you said rather than look at you. I remember Lewis commenting that Tolkien had said that someone wasn't looking very well and that he hadn't noticed at all. In any case, my first impressions of Tolkien was that he was a deeply sympathetic man and unselfish.

As this year is both the centenary of Lewis's birth and the twenty-fifth anniversary of Tolkien's death, would you summarize what you feel is their legacy?

Above all, they were both aware that the type of books they were writing were the type of books they liked to read. As Lewis said on one occasion: 'I wrote the sort of books I did because they were the sort of books I would have liked to have read when I was growing up.' When Lewis came across *The Hobbit* when it was being written he was delighted. This was not only the sort of book he would have liked to have read, but also the sort of book he would like to write. Back in the 1920s when Tolkien and Lewis had first met, and Tolkien started going to Lewis's rooms at Magdalen, Tolkien began reading parts of *The Silmarillion*. This was in 1929 and when Lewis heard it he was aghast. This was the sort of writing which he would not have dared to believe could exist. Then, as they drew closer and closer, they began to realize that they had so much to share. I think that Lewis was a great appreciator of Tolkien; and Tolkien of course was a great appreciator of Lewis. After all he was the one who pressed the publishers to accept *Out of the Silent Planet*. In effect, he got it published. This was the first one and very important in Lewis's life, the first work of fiction.

They were very honest men. They were not writing to be *avant garde*. They were writing books that they liked. They, after all, had jobs which left them free so they weren't depending on writing stories that would sell. In some respects, Tolkien was reluctant to send his work to a publisher so you can hardly call him ambitious for that type of success. They merely wrote the sort of books that they liked which turns out to be the sort of books that many other people like.

Why do you feel that the success of both Tolkien and Lewis in last year's Waterstones poll of the 'greatest book of the century' was greeted with such hostility by literary critics?

Well, the danger that Lewis and Tolkien now face is that so much has been learned about their lives that people who are antithetical to Christianity are forewarned of them, and even without reading their books these people know that Lewis and Tolkien are tarred with the Christian brush. These critics are totally against religion. I have come to discover that Marx was totally wrong when he said that religion is the opiate of the people. It may have seemed so to him at that time and he may have had reason to say what he did, but I think he would change his tune and say instead that atheism is the opium of the politically correct. I think there is general crowing about, and pride in, not being a Christian today. As a result, the mere fact that Tolkien and Lewis are Christians is a mark against them with the politically correct.

Do you think that many of the critics who derided Tolkien's and Lewis's success in the Waterstones poll would have done so without even reading their books?

I would have thought so, yes. I think political correctness is beginning to take on many of the traits of a religion. It is becoming very dogmatic, it is about certain doctrines that you seem to have to believe.

In spite of this, do you feel that Lewis and Tolkien should be seen primarily as Christian writers?

I think one of the most illuminating comments I have ever heard about Lewis was from someone who hadn't met him but who could understand human motivation very well and who also was a writer, and that was the Pope. I met him in 1984, and as I understand it the meeting was at his suggestion because he was the one who wanted to talk about Lewis. John Paul had been reading the works of Lewis at least since the fifties. Anyway, it was a great moment for me when I had the talk with him and he began by asking me, 'Do you still love your old friend C. S. Lewis?' I said, 'Yes, Holy Father, both *storge* and *philia*,' and he said, 'Ah, you knew I liked *The Four Loves*!' But at the end of the interview he then made a comment about Lewis. He said, 'C. S. Lewis *knew* what his apostolate was.' There was a long pause, then he said, 'And he *did* it!' I've been thinking about that ever since that time. What a judicious compliment that is! He knew what his apostolate was. Lots of people might know what their apostolate is, but he *did* it. And that brings in Tolkien's conscience. He was driven by conscience. Tolkien and Lewis both felt that if they *could* do it, they *ought* to do it.

I think both men shared something which is very unusual and we hardly know how to talk about it because it's so rare. They wrote with breathtaking clarity. They wrote different kinds of things but equally with breathtaking clarity. Tolkien in writing description is so memorable. It is more like the real world almost than the real world. And Lewis, writing theologically, could write with a clarity which made one feel that this cannot be profound because one never associates clarity with profundity. Yet, in passage after passage, we get this breathtaking clarity about things which are exceedingly profound as, for instance, when he said that we cannot speak of Jesus as a merely moral teacher. A man who was a merely moral teacher who said that he was the Son of God would be on a level with the man who said he was a poached egg or else he would be on the level with the devil of Hell; or he would be who he says he is. But don't let us come to him with any of that patronizing nonsense about Jesus being purely a moral teacher because he's not left that open to us. That's where you get the profundity and the clarity and it almost makes you laugh when you hear it because you suddenly have a profound truth present in your mind and it's clear. No one ever says, can you read that again so that I can understand it? You catch it the first time.

Do you feel that this combination of clarity and profundity, managing to convey the profound in a way which is crystal clear, is the secret of the success of both writers?

That's certainly part of it. Lewis and Tolkien wrote romances but Lewis found that one of the values of romances – mountains, giants, dragons – was that these are an 'admirable hieroglyphic' for types of people which succeed better as hieroglyphics than the characterization of a man. In writing to a child who had written to him about the Narnian stories, he was prompted to look at the relationship between all of these things and realism. He wrote that

> a strict allegory is like a puzzle with the solution. A great romance is like a flower whose smell reminds you of something you can't quite place. I think the 'something' is the whole quality of life as we actually experience it. You can have a realistic story in which all the things and people are exactly like those we meet in real life but the quality, feel, texture, smell of it is not. In a great romance it is just the opposite. I never met orcs, or ents, or elves but the feel of it, the sense of a huge past, of lowering danger, of heroic tasks achieved by the most apparently unheroic

people, of distance, vastness, strangeness, homeliness, all blended together, is so exactly what living feels like to me, particularly in the heartbreaking quality in the most beautiful places like Lothlórien, and it is so like the real history of the world.

And he quotes Tolkien: 'Then, as now, there was a growing darkness and great deeds were done that were not wholly in vain.' Neither optimism – 'this is the last war and after it all will be lovely for ever' – nor pessimism – 'this is the last war and all civilization will end'. No, the darkness comes again and again and it's never wholly triumphant nor wholly defeated. So from these great romances, the Narnias, the science fiction set in the heavens, Middle-earth, we get *more* reality into people's heads than you get from the copies of 'real life' that teach us nothing and that we remember nothing about. In these works of Lewis and Tolkien we have a *feel* that you just can't get anywhere else. It is similar to the way that some portrait painters are able to put into a portrait more of a man than a photograph can get. A photograph gets only something which existed for a second when the light was just so, whereas the portrait painter gives us something far more of the man as he is through many, many moments and years.

Why do you feel that the books of Lewis and Tolkien continue to sell in such great quantities?

Yes, who is buying Lewis's books now? This is a question which interests me very much. Well, I think I can say with absolute confidence that more and more Catholics are buying his books now because most of the translations that I've seen in recent years, particularly the Narnia stories, have come from Catholic countries. In many instances it is Catholic publishers who are translating Lewis, as in Italy. The same is true in Spain where the translations are the work of Opus Dei – so we know that Catholics are reading them in vast numbers throughout the world. We know also of course that there are a great many Protestants who read Lewis but I think there is a shift since he died insofar as he is read a great deal by the evangelical Protestants and less and less by the liberals. I don't think you would find that as many average Anglicans read him – not liberal Anglicans, they wouldn't read him. I was surprised to see what used to be a very Anglo-Catholic magazine from America now saying 'why did we ever read Lewis, he's far too doctrinal, he's far too Roman Catholic for us now'. But there are still many Protestants out there, in this country and in the United States and many other countries, who admire Lewis for the same reason that the Catholics do. They are supernaturalists and they need him as their ally in this battle. Lewis said in *Mere Christianity* that Christianity is a fighting religion and it looks as though only the evangelical Protestants and the Catholics are willing to get their hands dirty and fight. But the battle must have many soldiers in it because the number of Lewis's books which are read today is far in excess of anything that happened in his own lifetime.

Lewis and Tolkien both had apostolates which become clearer and clearer as time goes on. The Pope saw what Lewis's apostolate was and I think that Tolkien also had a very clear apostolate. He did what he should have done. He was a dutiful, good man and he lived the life that was given to him nobly and heroically but even he couldn't see how much he'd mean to people after he died. But we do, and I hope he forever knows how grateful we are.

Finally, as this volume of essays is entitled Tolkien: A Celebration, *what do you feel are the aspects of Tolkien's life and work which are most worth celebrating?*

The Lord of the Rings. I'm grateful for all of his works but I agree with Lewis that Tolkien's greatest achievement was *The Lord of the Rings*. I remember a letter that Lewis wrote to someone who read the newspapers and he said 'if you must read newspapers and magazines at least give yourself a mouthwash with *The Lord of the Rings*'. I think we all read newspapers and magazines and see this horrid modern language, and we're used to shoddy writing and shoddy imagining, and I think we all need one great book to have a mouthwash with, once a year. It's absolutely required.

INDEX

Also by Joseph Pearce and available from HarperCollins *Publishers*:

Tolkien: Man and Myth

A Literary Life

Tolkien may be the most popular writer of our age, but he is often misunderstood. This major new study of his life, his character and his work reveals the facts and confronts the myths. It explores the background to the man and the culture in which he wrote.

Tolkien: Man and Myth observes the relationships that the master writer had with his closest literary colleagues. It reveals his uneasy relationship with C. S. Lewis, the writer of the Narnia books, and the roots of their estrangement.

In this original book about a leading literary life, Joseph Pearce enters the world created by Tolkien in the seven books published during his lifetime. He explores the significance of Middle-earth and what it represented in Tolkien's thinking. Myth, to him, was not a leap from reality but a leap into reality.

Other aspects of his fascinating life troubled Tolkien greatly. The impact of his great notoriety, his relationship with material possessions and his traditional religious faith are all explored, making it possible to understand both the man and the myth he created.

Literary Converts

Spiritual Inspiration in an Age of Unbelief

The twentieth century has been marked both by belief and unbelief. While church attendance has declined, the lives of many of the most salient figures of our times have been influenced and inspired by Christianity.

Literary Converts is a biographical exploration into the spiritual lives of some of those figures. More specifically, it takes us on a journey into the deepest beliefs of some of the greatest writers in the English language: Oscar Wilde, Evelyn Waugh, C. S. Lewis, Malcolm Muggeridge, Graham Greene, Edith Sitwell, Siegfried Sassoon, Hilaire Belloc, G. K. Chesterton, Dorothy Sayers, T. S. Eliot and J. R. R. Tolkien. The role of George Bernard Shaw and H. G. Wells in intensifying the religious debate despite not being converts themselves is also considered.

Many will be intrigued to know more about what inspired their literary heroes; others will find the association of such names with Christian belief surprising or even controversial. Whatever viewpoint we may have, *Literary Converts* touches on some of the most important questions of the twentieth century, making it a fascinating read.